BECOMING

CRITICAL

RESEARCHERS

Studies in the
Postmodern Theory of Education

Joe L. Kincheloe and Shirley R. Steinberg
General Editors

Vol. 227

PETER LANG
New York • Washington, D.C./Baltimore • Bern
Frankfurt am Main • Berlin • Brussels • Vienna • Oxford

Ernest Morrell

BECOMING
CRITICAL
RESEARCHERS

Literacy
and Empowerment
for Urban Youth

PETER LANG
New York • Washington, D.C./Baltimore • Bern
Frankfurt am Main • Berlin • Brussels • Vienna • Oxford

Library of Congress Cataloging-in-Publication Data

Morrell, Ernest.
Becoming critical researchers: literacy and
empowerment for urban youth / Ernest Morrell.
p. cm. — (Counterpoints; vol. 227)
Includes bibliographical references (p.) and index.
1. Education, Urban—California, Southern—Case studies.
2. Urban youth—Education (Secondary)—California, Southern—
Case studies. 3. Literacy—California, Southern—Case studies.
4. Multicultural education—California, Southern—
Case studies. 5. Critical pedagogy. I. Title.
II. Counterpoints (New York, N.Y.); v. 227.
LC5132.C2M67   302.2'244—dc21   2003046085
ISBN 0-8204-6199-7
ISSN 1058-1634

Bibliographic information published by **Die Deutsche Bibliothek**.
Die Deutsche Bibliothek lists this publication in the "Deutsche
Nationalbibliografie"; detailed bibliographic data is available
on the Internet at http://dnb.ddb.de/.

Cover design by Dutton & Sherman Design

© 2004 Peter Lang Publishing, Inc., New York
275 Seventh Avenue, 28th Floor, New York, NY 10001
www.peterlangusa.com

Printed in the United States of America

For Jodene and Amani
My reasons for hope

CONTENTS

PART II
Ethnography

PART III
Lessons and Implications

ACKNOWLEDGMENTS

First of all, a special thanks to the students of the "Pacific Beach Project," for inspiring this study and these words. Next, I would like to acknowledge the faculty and students of UC Berkeley and UCLA for being good friends, colleagues, and mentors throughout this project. Finally, I need to thank grandma for the best pep talk ever and Jodene and Amani, who daily remind me of why this is all worthwhile.

I

INTRODUCTION, THEORY, METHOD, AND CONTEXT

1

INTRODUCTION

By nearly every statistical measure, urban students, particularly urban students of color, are trailing their suburban counterparts in academic achievement (Darling-Hammond, 1998; Fine, 1991; Kozol, 1991; Ladson-Billings, 1994; Jencks and Phillips, 1998). Although there have been marginal increases in achievement, a noticeable gap remains. This "achievement gap" is manifested through dropout rates, standardized test scores, advanced placement exams, and college eligibility indexes. A host of theories have been offered to explain this phenomenon, including poverty (Coleman et al., 1966; Jencks, 1972; Phillips et al., 1998; Wilson, 1996), cultural deficits (Bennett, 1994; Bourdieu, 1984; Payne, 1984), and a resistance toward school as an oppressive institution (Giroux, 1983; Kohl, 1991; MacLeod, 1987; Ogbu, 1994). Theorists such as Hernstein and Murray (1994) have gone so far as to attribute the inequality to genetic differences in intelligence.

In my early experiences as an urban high school teacher I saw firsthand how intelligent and motivated young people were alienated and disempowered by traditional curricula and pedagogical practices. A majority of my students had limited exposure to academic language and the themes and topics covered in academic texts. When placed in classrooms where they were provided culturally irrelevant or alienating texts and confronted with disempowering pedagogies, these students reported feeling distanced, uninterested, or worse yet, angry and bitter at the institutions that created these oppressive conditions. These experiences have been corroborated through countless other research projects focusing on low-income, low-tracked students of color attempting to navigate the traditional, college-bound curriculum (Fine, 1991; Lee, 1992; MacLeod, 1987; Oakes, 1985).

At the same time, however, I observed these same students exhibiting the critical and analytical skills that would serve them well in class when engaging popular culture and discussing issues pertinent to their everyday lives as young people attempting to navigate an often hostile world. I was intrigued but still unable to decrease the gap between student ability and student achievement. Frustration and feelings of failure led me back to a graduate program in language, literacy, and culture. I needed answers. Through my engagement with social, critical, cultural, sociocultural, and literacy theories, I came to understand that students are learners and powerful users of language and literacy as participants in cultural communities. I also began to understand that I could draw upon students' background knowledge and expertise to help them gain the understanding and confidence they needed to navigate traditional academic texts as well as become conscious of and enhance their critical perspectives. Once I was able to construct the students as holders and producers of relevant classroom knowledge, whole worlds opened up for my practice.

I also began to understand that schools were institutions that played a major role in promoting social inequality. Far from being the "great equalizers" they were intended to be (Tyack, 1974), schools were often segregated (Kozol, 1991; Orfield, 1996) and provided differential instruction to students (Oakes, 1985). I was inspired, though, to think of schooling as a place not only to increase academic knowledge, but, through counterhegemonic curricula (Apple, 1990) and critical teaching practices (Freire, 1997), also to foster awareness of social issues in empowering students to transform them. I was further inspired to conceptualize learning as a social practice that involved activity and not the passive transmission of knowledge from a knowing teacher to ignorant students. Authentic learning, then, would involve apprenticeship (Rogoff, 1990) and legitimate participation in relevant sociocultural activity (Lave and Wenger, 1991). By allowing students to study what was around them, and by imparting the tools of investigation, inquiry, and analysis, I could make schooling become an act of resistance in developing agency and a commitment to action. This process, I gathered, could also be used to promote the development of academic competencies.

This book reports the findings of a multiyear critical ethnography I conducted with urban students, which drew upon many of these principles, theoretical frameworks, and hypotheses. I attempted to understand the relationship between apprenticing urban youth as critical researchers of popular culture, the everyday experiences of marginalized peoples, and the development of academic and critical literacies. Although each of these terms will be defined and articulated at length throughout the study, I want to offer preliminary definitions of the terms "academic literacy" and "critical literacy." By academic literacy, I simply mean those forms of engaging, producing, and dialoguing about texts that have currency in primary, secondary, and postsecondary education (Harris and Hodges, 1995; Street, 1993; Venezky et al., 1990). It is important to note, however, that changing technologies and the onset of new (computer, cyber, digital, technical, video, visual) literacies are changing what it means to be academically literate (Alvermann, 2001; Cushman, Kingten, Kroll and Rose, 2000). Also, critical literacy theorists explicitly challenge the notion of academic literacy as being laden with dominant ideologies which privilege some groups while marginalizing others. These caveats, though, do not rule out the importance of understanding or even promoting academic literacy development as critical educators seek to both problematize and expand the meaning of the term.

Critical literacy has been defined as the ability to not only read and write, but to assess texts in order to understand the relationships between power and domination that underlie and inform them (Hull, 1993). Critical literacy can also illuminate the power relationships in society and encourage those who are critically literate to participate in and use literacy to change dominant power structures to liberate those who are oppressed by them (Freire and Macedo, 1987). Those who are critically literate are able to understand the socially constructed meaning embedded in texts as well as the political and economic contexts in which texts are embedded. Ultimately, critical literacy can lead to an emancipated worldview and even transformative social action (Freire, 1970; Hull, 1993; McLaren, 1989; UNESCO, 1975).

Using a sociocultural lens, which views learning as changing participation over time (Lave and Wenger, 1991; Wenger, 1998), I developed a coordinated, multiyear ethnography to evaluate the impact of students' movement from peripheral to full participation in a critical research community of practice on the development of academic and critical literacies. I also wanted to evaluate the students' abilities to translate these newly acquired identities and literacies into increased academic performance, greater access to college, and commitment to social action. The study itself was conducted during the two school years and summers that I spent working on a college access project with urban students of color at Pacific Beach, a bimodal high school in Southern California.

Delpit (1988) suggested that educators needed to make explicit the rules of the culture of power for poor and minority students. In order to accomplish this, however, teachers must understand the cultural frames of reference of the students they teach (Foster, 1998; Ladson-Billings, 1994; Lee, 1992; Mahiri, 1998). Without a sufficient understanding of students' cultures and histories, it is almost impossible for teachers to tap into the funds of knowledge that these students, as members of multiple cultures and communities, already possess (Moll, 2000). This is compatible with a Vygotskian perspective that views optimal learning as taking place within a "zone of proximal development"; that is, a space beyond what the students can do alone, but not beyond their potential growth with expert assistance (Vygotsky, 1978). If teachers are to be experts, they need knowledge of students' cultures in order to be able to meet them within this zone (Lee and Smagorinsky, 2000).

This study explores methods of bridging the gap between urban students' cultural frames of reference and the culture of power through an examination of the potential of incorporating the critical study of popular culture into traditional curricula. The goals are to discover ways to provide greater access to the traditional texts with which the students will need to be familiar in order to approach standard examinations and college coursework, and to provide a greater understanding of urban, youth, and popular cultures while also fostering a critical perspective, an empowered identity, and a commitment to social action.

I developed four sets of questions. Each set of questions deals with a different unit of analysis, including the student, the classroom, the teacher, and the school:

1. Questions dealing with the student: What is the potential of engaging urban students in critical research relating to popular culture to facilitate the development of academic and critical literacies? How can this approach provide students with the confidence and skills they need to critically analyze literary texts from the canon and college-level texts in general? How can this approach enable students to critique the social institutions and popular cultural media that permeate their everyday life?
2. Questions dealing with the classroom: How can an understanding of sociocultural theory and critical pedagogy be incorporated to create critical learning communities that facilitate literacy development in classrooms where urban students are engaged as critical researchers?
3. Questions dealing with the teacher: What skills, sensitivities, background knowledge, theoretical foundations, and ideology do teachers need in order to be successful in engaging urban students in critical research relating to popular cultures?
4. Questions dealing with the school: What roles can schools play in either limiting or facilitating a climate of critical research? What aspects of the structure of schools, including the traditional and hidden curricula, serve as barriers to creating critical research communities? How might we envision schools as operating differently and being more receptive of these new relationships, activities, and work products?

Outline of the Book

Chapter 2 draws upon multiple theoretical perspectives to create the foundation for curricula and pedagogical practices that problematize dominant hegemony, employ definitions of culture that include mass, youth, and popular cultures, and seek to engage urban youth as intellectuals, street sociologists, and critical researchers while simultaneously increasing the development of academic and critical literacies. I locate this work both within and in contention against the major tenets of multicultural education. That is, I agree that curricula need to be relevant to the lived cultural experiences of students and, in ideal conditions, draw upon and affirm the lived experiences of students. I argue, however, that it is necessary to move away from conceptions of students as monocultural beings and of cultures as synonymous with essentialized racial or ethnic identities.

It is important at this point to pause and define two terms that will be central to the study, namely, "culture" and "popular culture." Williams (1995) suggests that culture is one of the most complex terms in the English language. Critiquing sociologists, anthropologists, and "cultural" critics who examine only single components of culture, Williams (1998) articulates three components of culture that are essential to any thorough analysis of the subject. The first of these components is the *ideal*, in which culture is a state or process human perfection in terms of absolute or universal values. The analysis of culture in this vein is essentially the discovery and description, in lives and works, of those values which can be seen to compose a timeless order, or to have permanent reference to the universal human condition (Williams, 1998, p. 48).

According to the *documentary* component, culture is the body of intellectual and imaginative work in which human thought and experience is recorded. Here, an analysis of culture proceeds through the activity of criticism, in which the nature of thought and experience and the details of the language, form, and convention in which these are active are described, deconstructed and ultimately valued or devalued (Williams, 1998, p. 48).

The third, or *social,* component of culture is a description of a particular way of life, which expresses certain meanings and values not only in art and learning, but also in institutions and "ordinary" behavior. The analysis of culture, here, means the clarification of the meanings and values implicit and explicit in particular ways of life, in a particular culture. It also includes analysis of the organization of production, the structure of the family, the structure of institutions that express or govern social relationships, and the characteristic forms through which members of the society communicate (Williams, 1998, p. 48).

Each of these components is represented in this analysis of critical researchers of popular culture. In the *ideal* component, this analysis examines popular culture as it relates to the expression of universal human values, namely, the desire and struggle for freedom from tyranny and oppression. It also *documents* and analyzes elements of the body of intellectual and imaginative work that comprise popular culture, such as hip-hop music, and artifacts associated with the mainstream media. Finally, it examines popular culture as the everyday *social* experiences of marginalized students as they confront, make sense of, and contend against social institutions such as schools (Bowles and Gintis, 1976), the mass media (Baudrillard, 1994), corporations, and governments (Giddens, 1987).

My definition of popular culture is inspired by cultural theorists (Docker, 1994; Hall, 1998; McCarthy, 1998; Storey, 1998), who were themselves inspired by Williams, by critical theorists (Adorno and Horkheimer, 1999), and by the Marxist social theorist Antonio Gramsci (1971). These theorists see popular culture as a site of struggle between the forces of resistance of subordinate groups in society and the forces of incorporation of dominant groups in society. Popular culture, they argue, is neither an imposed mass culture, nor a people's culture; it is more of a terrain of exchange between the two. The texts and practices of popular culture move within what Gramsci (1971) calls a compromise equilibrium. Those who look at popular culture from the neo-Gramscian perspective tend to see it as a terrain of ideological struggle between dominant and subordinate classes, or dominant and subordinate cultures, expressed through music, film, mass media artifacts, language, customs, and values.

Chapter 3 outlines the epistemological and methodological foundations of the study. Employing a cultural studies epistemology that draws upon critical theory, postmodernism, and Marxism, this critical ethnography is designed to capture literacy events that demonstrate academic mastery and critical consciousness (Carspecken, 1996; Kincheloe and McLaren, 1998). I follow Carspecken, Kincheloe, and McLaren in their argument that research must not only benefit the researcher but also empower the objects of the research. When applying this philosophy to my own work, I see it as important that the students involved become empowered through their increased academic skills, but also in gaining a critical awareness of the role that societal institutions (i.e. schools and the media) play in reproducing social inequality. In chapter 3, I explain my rationale for selecting a critical ethnographic methodology and briefly describe the site and the participants. I also explain the selection of the focal students, and I introduce the focal students, the focal teachers, and the focal school. Further, I discuss the data collection and data analysis, and I conclude with a reflection on my social location as a researcher.

In chapter 4, I combine an examination of historical documents and interviews with my observations, to construct a narrative of the evolution of Pacific Beach[1] into its present population of affluent Anglos combined with working-class Latinos and African-Americans who are relegated to a small corridor in the town. I also examine the "liberal ethos" of the town and the way that ethos manifests itself in the school district, which closely mirrors the demographics of the State of California. Further, I look at the implications of this history and diversity on academic achievement at Pacific Beach High School. I focus on the disparity in achievement between the affluent white/Asian population and the working-class African-American/Latino population, and I explain how the Pacific Beach Project was designed to address some of these inequities.

Chapters 5 through 8 follow four focal students over a two-year period to determine the impact, on their literacy development, of being apprenticed as critical researchers of youth and popular cultures. I examine "student learning," which, following sociocultural theorists (Cole, 1996; Lave and Wenger, 1991; Rogoff, 1990; Vygotsky, 1978; Wenger, 1998), I am defining as changing in participation over time in sociocultural activity. As the students move from legitimate peripheral participation to more core participation as social theorists and critical researchers (Lave and Wenger, 1991), I document how this student learning (i.e., changing participation) impacts the students' ability to engage and produce powerful texts.

Chapter 5 follows the focal students' participation in a three-week summer research seminar held at a local university. In this seminar, the students were invited to read seminal works in the sociology of education and participate in a set of

---

1. Pacific Beach is a pseudonym.

mini-research projects around the broad theme of "Race, Class, and Access in American Education." Over the course of three intensive weeks of study, the focal students worked in five-member teams to produce a piece of original research that they presented to a panel of university faculty members with expertise in the area of educational sociology. Through interviews with affiliated faculty and analyses of student work, this chapter examines the relationship between legitimate peripheral participation and literacy development.

Perhaps the most important outcome of the summer research seminar was that the students began to see themselves as intellectuals and as researchers. They also saw youth and urban issues as worthy of serious study (by urban youth themselves) and saw that research could have both a social origin and a social impact. Throughout the remainder of their high school careers, these students would struggle to create links between their research and academic advancement. They would also use their new knowledge and new identities to challenge social injustice in their school and in their communities, all the while becoming more core participants in a critical research focused community of practice and reading and writing in powerful ways.

Chapter 6 follows the focal students as they returned to Pacific Beach High for their 11th-grade year. When the 1999–2000 school year was beginning, the project research team felt compelled to design a program that honored and built upon the experience of the summer seminar. After we observed the transformation in participation, work products, and identities associated with legitimate peripheral participation, we found it impossible to return to a school year of business as usual. Several major changes were made, to allow for the changing participation of the youth who were apprenticing as critical researchers of popular cultures. First of all, we designed an A period class (one that meets before school) to allow students to further develop their summer research projects and to begin new work in the school context. Also, opportunities were created for students to present their research findings in guest lectures to graduate students, to preservice teachers, to practicing teachers who were participants in a regional writing conference, and to teachers at Pacific Beach High. Further, students were frequently taken to local universities and other locations for research and activism-related activities. They were given the opportunity to collect data for their research and interact with core participants in these communities. Finally, a majority of the students enrolled in the English sections ("regular" English 11 or English 11 AP) of Ms. Weiss (a focal teacher and Project team member) where they were able to rely on their community of practice and draw upon their knowledge of social theory and critical research to interrogate classical and contemporary literature and develop as expository writers.

To exemplify the changes in participation over this school year, I draw upon data from a hip-hop documentary that two of the focal students attended as well as a protest against a racist video game. I also document how preparation for and participation in the final exams of the project class honored the new positioning of the students while furthering their research projects and developing academic and critical literacies. Finally, I choose several examples where students draw upon their participation in a research community of practice to assist their progress in traditional academic courses.

Chapter 7 follows the focal students through their second summer seminar course at the university, "Education, Access, and Democracy in Los Angeles: LA Youth and Convention 2000." During the first two weeks of the course, the students received background information in critical research, political conventions as narratives, and the key issues affecting participants inside and outside the convention. Students also began working within their research groups, framing questions, reading literature, and collecting preliminary data. During the third week of the four-week seminar, students met at a church in a downtown neighborhood and participated in the Democratic National Convention. Students visited Staples Center, the Shadow Convention, and the designated Protest Area and collected data for their research projects. During the final week of the seminar, the students returned to the university where they began data analysis and prepared to present their findings to a university faculty panel, community activists, high school faculty, and family members.

In honoring the students' changing participation in this community of practice, several changes were made in the design of the seminar. Whereas the Summer Seminar of 1999 met for a total of 25 classroom hours (2 hours per day for 12 days), the Summer Seminar of 2000 would meet for nearly 80 hours (4 hours a day for 20 days). The students as experienced researchers were given a more rigorous reading list and more was expected of them as they engaged the literature. The seminar also focused more heavily on critical writing, including daily reflective journals and group papers to accompany the presentations. Further, the students were given time to "go into the field" to gather data in and around the Democratic National Convention (DNC). In contrast to the previous summer when the data collection sites were firmly controlled, the students had virtually free rein during the convention and were encouraged to record observations and interview participants. Finally, students were provided with laptop computers to use throughout the seminar to aid in their research, taught how to use the Internet as a site to collect data for their critical research projects, and encouraged to communicate through cyberspace.

The second summer research seminar provided the focal students with an opportunity to focus exclusively on critical research in a supportive environment containing core participants in the practice of critical research. All of the students were, at this stage, becoming experts at research and used this expertise to further develop as readers, writers, speakers, activists, and critical citizens. In particular, the students began to produce more critical writing surrounding their research enterprise. They also used writing more creatively to impact their audience. Students also publicly struggled with one another to convert what they were learning from social theory into social critique and social action. Through the presentation of ethnographic narratives (Berg, 2001), I illustrate how this changing participation manifested itself during the summer at the DNC and its impact on further promoting academic and critical literacy development for the students involved.

Chapter 8 follows the focal students through their final year at Pacific Beach High School. There were several key transformations in the students as they emerged from the Summer Research Seminar 2000 and began to move toward more core participation as critical researchers of urban, youth, and popular cultures. The students found sites to publish and present their own work, they took the initiative to collect and analyze their own data, and they continued to write and research extensively as participants in the project courses.

In addition to the literacy development, it is also important to examine the relationship between core participation and becoming agents of change. Several focal students joined the Associated Student Body as elected officers and representatives for their senior years, one took the initiative to start a women's group that aimed to empower young women of color in the Rivera (working-class) neighborhood of Pacific Beach, one organized a conference at the school for men of color and participated as an organizer of the annual Racial Harmony Retreat, while another traveled to the east coast and to the San Francisco Bay Area to present her research. All of the students became instrumental in establishing a partnership with a research cohort in Northern California and initiating crucial conversations with the on-site and district administration, where they used their research, knowledge of theory, and personal experiences to speak to the nature of schooling for low-income students of color. As full participants, the students also established an ongoing dialogue with the American Civil Liberties Union (ACLU), which was involved in litigation regarding educational inequalities and they also regularly addressed groups of graduate students and preservice teachers at local universities.

Over a period of two years, the focal students and their peers in the Pacific Beach Project changed from novices learning the basics of critical research and social theory into productive writers, researchers, and speakers who published their work, gave guest lectures, pursued independent research projects, and used critical research as a form of social action. They were also deemed by experienced academics as estimable colleagues whose research was valuable to the sociology of education. As their participation changed with movement from peripheral toward full participation in a critical research community of practice, Jaime, Luz, Wanda, and Imani were able to develop the literacies needed to be successful as postsecondary students, as scholars, and as critical citizens. As the students moved toward full participation in this research community, they read more complex works and read those works more critically; produced more powerful theoretical and analytical writing; presented their research with greater creativity, sophistication, and confidence; and developed other literacies (cyber-literacy and digital-literacy) which were important to both academic achievement and critical citizenship (Alvermann, 2001). These students also came to a greater understanding of critical social theory, wrestled with how to combine their knowledge of theory with an agenda of social action, participated in social action, and saw themselves as critical researchers and social activists.

Chapter 9 outlines the logic of social reproduction at Pacific Beach High School, offering several examples of how this logic played out in the experiences of the low-income students of color involved in the Pacific Beach Project. It also analyzes several poignant moments of conflict where project participants attempted to challenge or subvert this logic. Finally, it evaluates the ultimate impact of the project on the structure and culture of Pacific Beach High School, while offering suggestions for an agenda of large-scale equity-minded school reform that empowers marginalized students and families and is compatible with the mission of the project and the findings of preliminary research.

While I was performing research on the students and teachers associated with the Pacific Beach Project, it became more and more evident to me that the school played a major role in countering and even subverting the critical enterprise of the project and also the ability of marginalized students to acquire academic and critical literacies. Rarely overt or explicit, these constraining actions, perpetuated by administrators, teachers, counselors, or parents, were described or defended as logical behavior (MacLeod, 1987; Willis, 1977). The sum total of these actions, I argue, was the perpetuation of social reproduction at Pacific Beach High School.

It became increasingly important in my research project to determine the role that a seemingly "logical" school structure and culture played in thwarting the efforts of students who had demonstrated the academic competencies needed for success at this comprehensive high school and in postsecondary education. It was also important to locate concentrated efforts to subvert the logic of the school and to evaluate the relative impact of these moments of conflict. I provide examples of the logic of social reproduction at the high school, show evidence of the project's attempts to disrupt this logic, and evaluate the impact of the project on transforming reproductive school structures and cultures.

Chapter 10 revisits the research questions and offers implications of the study for urban educators, administrators, teacher educators, and policymakers. It closes by presenting a vision of a new Pacific Beach High School that opens up spaces for authentic dialogue, new forms of participation, and curricular projects that are immediately relevant to the lives of urban youth.

2

THEORY

"Culturally" Relevant Instruction in the Postmodern Landscape

Cultural theorists critique and complicate modernist uses of culture and race (McCarthy, 1998) and call for a sociological definition of culture (Williams, 1998) that encompasses mass, youth, and popular cultures. This chapter draws upon various theoretical lenses that highlight the historical, social, economic, and cultural contexts of urban schools as simultaneously sites of reproduction and resistance. It also looks to critical educational theory, which calls for pedagogical practices that facilitate the empowerment of marginalized students as critical intellectuals. It engages new literacy theories, which respect and legitimate the literacy practices of marginalized students in nonschool settings, and it also engages situated learning theories that view learning as movement from legitimate peripheral participation to full participation in communities of practice.

McCarthy (1998) critiques terms such as race, identity, and culture as highly decentered and decentering social constructs—the products of historical center-periphery relations and consequent processes of hybridization. In making the argument for cultural hybridity, he points to the war over culture between Great Britain and the United States, which he experienced while attending school on a former British colonial island. According to McCarthy, there is no one unified definition of whiteness or of Western thought. Similarly, there is nothing pure about being black or African:

There is nothing original: all is intertextuality, rearticulation, translation. There is no transcendent core: all is epidermis. All is movement on the Black Atlantic. The sound and fury of race signifies everything and nothing. (1998, p. 11)

McCarthy (1998) critiques the tendency in current liberal and neo-Marxist writing on race and gender to treat social groups as stable or homogeneous entities or to locate the "source" of racial differences in schooling in a single variable or cause. Racial categories, he argues, have been seen as immutable and are taken for granted even though history has revealed "race" to be a modern social construction.

McCarthy also seeks to promote a rethinking of constructs such as culture and identity, and the relations between centers and peripheries. He argues that these concepts and relations are far more dynamic than the ways in which they are normally conceptualized in educational research. While scholars have attempted to fix and separate cultures in order to reform curricula, they have neglected both the historical and contemporary heterogeneity of human interactions and lives. In contrast, McCarthy argues that literature and popular culture both provide arenas in which cultural hybridity is displayed and even flaunted, through tropes such as parody and melancholy.

In questioning the current use of race and culture and challenging the idea of a center-periphery relationship, McCarthy (1998) makes the argument for multiple perspectives. In its relevance to marginalized peoples, his work supports the study of popular culture as an academic and critical enterprise. McCarthy tires of the usage of essentialized terms such as "race," "culture," "pure," and "hierarchy," and attempts to use the postcolonial gaze as a standpoint for problematizing and ultimately transcending these debilitating and confining terms. However, his work remains largely couched in the language he works so diligently to deconstruct.

There is a valid reason for McCarthy's inability to completely abandon the language of race in his analysis, namely, the continued significance of race in American life. West (1993), for example, argues that race still matters to a true analysis of access and equality in American society because power and access are still largely determined by one's (real or perceived) membership in a particular racial group. That is, race is real to the extent that those in power believe in race and act upon their beliefs. The continued existence of racial profiling and gaps in academic achievement, college enrollment, and performance on standardized assessments all point to the continued significance of race as a determinant of access. Further, many students still attend racially segregated schools (Kozol, 1991; Orfield, 1996) or, as in Pacific Beach, attend diverse schools where students are resegregated into upper and lower tracks and treated and taught differently because of their racial identity.

It is important, though, to separate an analysis of race as a real phenomenon from a critique of multicultural education programs that fail to acknowledge the social construction of race. The intent of this book is not to argue against the salience of race to unpacking the social reality, but to problematize pedagogical approaches that are centered upon race yet are uncritical of the concept or its uses. It is not contradictory to say that, although race is still paramount to our understanding of the world, critical educators need to move beyond its grasp when seeking new and powerful ways to educate members of marginalized groups. The critique that McCarthy offers, therefore, is an important one for researchers, educators, and policymakers concerned with diverse new century schools.

There are, however, many unanswered questions for critical educators who seek to educate for empowerment and access. How do we effectively educate marginalized students in a way that addresses the impact of race yet transcends the social construction of race (Davis, 1991; Marger, 1993; Omi and Winant, 1984) and unifies rather than divides? How can a critical pedagogy provide access to dominant institutions yet remain critical of these same institutions? How should critical pedagogists position themselves vis à vis urban students and communities to educate for empowerment and access? What theoretical frameworks/modes of inquiry offer the most potential for tackling these tough issues? I now turn toward social, critical, cultural, new literacy, and sociocultural theories to examine these questions and others in the process of situating a critical research community of practice involving urban teachers and students.

Social and Critical Educational Theories

Social educational theorists (Bowles and Gintis, 1976; Carnoy and Levin, 1985; MacLeod, 1987; Oakes, 1985; Willis, 1977) employ sociological theories of the state (defined as the government of a sovereign body) and its role in social reproduction to provide grounded explanations of the role that schools play in the reproduction of social inequality. Explicit theories of the state—explanations of how political agents interact, individually and collectively, vis-à-vis social structures and institutions—they argue, are lacking from most educational writing, even though public education is primarily a state function, and the state has become an increasingly significant part of the production system.

Education as part of the functions of the state is also an arena of social conflict. If the state in capitalist democracies is viewed as responsible for providing justice and equity to compensate for inequalities arising out of the social and economic system, education's role, then, is seen as improving the social position of have-not groups by making relevant knowledge and certification for participation available to them. At the same time the capitalist state and its educational system reproduce capitalist relations of production, including the division of labor and the class relations that are part of this division. The tension between reproducing inequality and producing greater equality is inherent in public schooling, just as social tension is inherent in all institutions structured according to class, race, and gender. The basis of this tension is not ideology as such, but ideology as it relates to the concrete reality of social position, material wealth, and political power.

The education system is the principal public institution organized for shaping youth into working adults, but schools are subject to conflicting forces over their purpose and operation. Public education both reproduces the unequal hierarchical relations of the nuclear family and the capitalist workplace and also presents opportunities for social mobility and the extension of democratic rights (Carnoy and Levin, 1985).

There are two levels at which the schools are involved in reproduction (Carnoy and Levin, 1985). At the first level, the school system's structure has developed in the context of capitalist production and class conflict. At the second level, school practices have attempted to produce general values and norms consistent with the reproduction of relations of production and differentiated behavior and knowledge for young people who are destined for different segments of the workforce. The class-based reproduction process attempts to prepare young people to accept capitalist development by reconciling themselves to their role in it (MacLeod, 1987). Reproduction theory implies that institutions of socialization (such as public schools) are such that someone from a lower social class is likely to acquire less schooling, obtain different knowledge, and work in lower-paying categories of occupation than someone with parents in highly skilled professional work (Bowles and Gintis, 1976).

Many historians, political economists, and reproduction theorists (Anyon, 1997; Carnoy and Levin, 1985; Tyack, 1974) situate contemporary urban schooling as a response to the turn of the twentieth century's rapid industrialization. Families and churches were no longer sufficient as the primary socializing agents of youth. Employers, the masters of the new industrial empire, pushed for an educational system that would teach people to accept their designated role in the production process and that would socialize young people into a class-stratified organization of production (Carnoy and Levin, 1985). Educational growth in the United States was conditioned by the class conflict underlying capitalist production and the changing nature of the workplace. Schools expanded as part of a production-centered historical dynamic in which they reproduced the developing conditions of capitalist production while simultaneously responding to the demands of labor and growing school bureaucracies. The growth of schooling is intertwined with the changing workplace and with social demands for upward mobility and increased democracy; the tensions created by such competing demands—tensions that until recently were sometimes eased by educational expansion itself—have continually shaped the role and structure of schooling.

Schools take the cultural capital, the habitus, of the dominant class as natural and employ it as if all children have had equal access to it (Bourdieu, 1986). However, by taking all children as equal, while implicitly favoring those who have already acquired the linguistic and social competencies to handle middle-class culture, schools take as natural what is essentially a social gift, that is, cultural capital. Schools, therefore, "process" both knowledge and people. In essence, formal and informal knowledge is used as a complex filter to process people, often by class. At the same time, different dispositions and values are taught to different school populations, again often by class (plus gender and race). In effect, for this more critical tradition, schools subtly recreate cultural and economic disparities, though this is certainly not what most school personnel intend at all (Apple, 1990). For clarification, one should look at the subtle connections between educational phenomena such as curriculum and the latent social and economic outcomes of the institution.

MacLeod's (1987) ethnographic study elucidates ways in which the structures and practices of comprehensive high schools serve to promote the social reproduction of inequality. It involves two disparate groups (the Brothers and the Hallway Hangers), residents in Clarendon Heights, a small housing project in a northeastern city. The Hallway Hangers, mostly Italian and Irish, were a trouble-causing lot that liked to smoke, fight, and hang out. The Brothers, mostly African-American, by comparison, were more respectful of authority and more interested in sports and girls than bravado. They possessed what MacLeod terms the achievement ideology: the belief that America is fair and full of opportunity and success is a result of merit. They also believed in the efficacy of schooling, that hard work and education translate into economic success. The Hallway Hangers had no such faith in the system and, therefore, opted out and acted out. Neither group achieves much success at Lincoln High School, which, although diverse, was heavily tracked. The Hallway Hangers exerted no effort to conform (except in Jimmy Sullivan's controversial "Adjustment Class") while the Brothers lacked the cultural capital (cultural background, knowledge, disposition, and skills) of the dominant class required for scholastic success. The Brothers were inclined to blame themselves for their lack of academic success (didn't try hard enough, were lazy, etc.), which fits with social reproduction theory (everyone in the fragmented class structure believes they got what they deserved).

Even though all of the Brothers graduated from high school, 10 years later they were either unemployed or working for barely above minimum wage. The only Brother to "make it out" was the white one (Michael) who had to resort to falsifying his educational history. All of the Hallway Hangers were into drugs (the two black ones most heavily), most had spent time in prison, and all were poor. MacLeod's ethnography documents the process of social reproduction in urban schools and demonstrates the various impacts of schooling on urban boys. His work, however, does not explicitly point toward a strategy of disrupting social reproduction, whereas critical educational theory has made this disruption a primary aim.

Critical educational theorists draw inspiration from the critical theorists of the Frankfurt School, such as Adorno, Horkheimer, Marcuse, and Habermas. Using a neo-Marxist-Hegelian framework in a modern context, these scholars developed a critical theory that sought to challenge the dominant discourse (hegemony), uncover the inherent bias in the "common sense" assumptions made by traditional theorists, challenge the existing theoretical paradigms, make explicit the correlation between existing sanctioned knowledge and existing power relations, commit intellectual activity to social transformation, and build in a system of self-reflection and critique.

Critical education theory, then, attempts to make sense of the impact that capitalism, mass culture, and totalizing modernist narratives have had on the creation and function of urban schooling and the subsequent inequities in educational attainment and the facilitation of social and cultural reproduction. It also looks to critical dialogue and revolutionary praxis among students and teachers as ways to transform urban education and, ultimately, the social order (McLaren, 1989; Freire, 1997; hooks, 1994; Shor, 1992).

Critical educational theorists look to critical pedagogies that engage students from marginalized backgrounds as subjects and intellectuals in liberating and transformative dialogue for the purpose of educational and social transformation (Apple, 1990; Aronowitz and Giroux, 1991; Darder, 1991; Freire, 1997; hooks, 1994; McLaren, 1989; Shor, 1992). Critical educational theorists also look to facilitate critical literacies, that is, a consciousness of the power relations in society and the role that language (and dominant cultures) play in maintaining inequities in these power relations (Freire and Macedo, 1987; Gee, 1995; Heath, 1983; Hull, 1993; Mahiri, 1998; Street, 1993).

Critical educational theorists promote critical media literacy. They encourage a consciousness of the corporate-controlled media's role as public pedagogue to create and market dominant narratives that serve the interests of the dominant class (Kellner, 1995; McLaren, 1995). Finally, critical educational theorists encourage members of marginalized groups and those that work with them to engage in critical research for the purpose of questioning existing power relations, facilitating consciousness, and transforming social institutions (i.e. schools) and the social order (Carspecken, 1996; Kincheloe and McLaren, 1998).

These theorists argue strongly that education is not a neutral enterprise, that by the very nature of the institution, the educator is involved, whether he or she is conscious of it or not, in a political act. Apple (1990) contends that educators and theorists must complement an economic analysis with an approach that leans more heavily on a cultural and ideological orientation if they are completely to understand the complex ways in which social, economic, and political tensions and contradictions are "mediated" in the concrete practices of schooling's participants as they go about their business. Not only is there an economic property, but there also seems to be a symbolic property—cultural capital—that schools preserve and distribute. Thus, through uncovering the relationship between ideology and schools' structures and practices, critical educators can acquire a more thorough understanding of how institutions of cultural preservation and distribution, like schools, create and recreate forms of consciousness that enable social control to be maintained without dominant groups having to resort to overt forms of domination. Apple asserts that educators need to examine critically not just how a student acquires more knowledge, but why and how particular aspects of the collective culture are presented in school as objective, factual knowledge. Apple also speaks of the hidden curriculum of schools, which he defines as the tacit teaching of norms, values, and dispositions that goes on simply as a result of living and coping with the institutional expectations and routines of schools day in and day out for a number of years. "In order to fully understand how schools function," he argues, "we must study schools as institutions that process knowledge, as institutions that serve an ideological function." (Apple, 1990, p. 15).

Educators have almost totally depoliticized the culture that schools distribute, passing off hegemonic curricula and pedagogies as neutral, value-free, and the only options for "doing school" (Apple, 1990; Giroux, 1988; McLaren, 1989). In response to this indoctrination there have emerged a growing number of critical curriculum scholars and sociologists of education (Apple, 1990; Aronowitz and Giroux, 1991; Bourdieu and Passeron, 1977; McLaren, 1989; MacLeod, 1987; Wexler, 1976) who are taking much more seriously these questions: Whose culture? What group's knowledge? And in whose interest is certain knowledge (facts, skills, propensities, and dispositions) taught in cultural institutions like schools? These scholars argue against taking it for granted that curricular knowledge is neutral; instead, they argue for unpacking the social interests—or ideologies—embodied in the knowledge forms themselves.

Functionally, ideology has been evaluated historically as a form of false consciousness that distorts one's picture of social reality and serves the interests of the dominant classes in a society (Marx, 1967). Sociologists tend to agree that ideology is associated with legitimization—the justification of group action and its social acceptance. Ideology seeks to sanctify existence by bringing it under the domination of ultimately right principles. Power conflict is always at stake in ideological disputes, whether or not those involved expressly acknowledge that dimension. An explicit and systematic rhetoric is also evident in the realm of ideology. Embracing the concept that ideological saturation permeates lived experiences allows critical subjects to see how people can employ frameworks that both assist them in organizing their world and enable them to believe they are neutral participants in the neutral instrumentation of schooling.

Thinking of schools as mechanisms of cultural distribution is important since, as Gramsci (1971) noted, a critical element in enhancing the ideological dominance of certain classes is the control of the knowledge-preserving and knowledge-producing institutions of a society. This concerns the relationship between the type of curricular knowledge that is accorded high status in our society and its economic and cultural effects. It is difficult to think through the past and present problems of the form and content of curriculum without attempting to uncover the complex nexus linking cultural and economic production (Bourdieu and Passeron, 1977). The language of learning is portrayed as apolitical and ahistorical, thus hiding the complex nexus of political and economic power and resources that lies behind a considerable amount of curriculum organization and selection.

The possession of high-status knowledge, knowledge that is considered of exceptional import and connected to the structure of corporate economies, is related to and in fact seems to entail its nonpossession by others (Apple, 1996). High-status knowledge is by definition scarce, and its scarcity is inextricably linked to its instrumentality. Just as in the economic marketplace, where it is more efficient to have a relatively constant level of unemployment, even to actually generate it, cultural institutions "naturally" generate levels of poor achievement. Apple (1996) argues that the distribution or scarcity of certain forms of cultural capital is of less importance in this calculus of values than the maximization of the production of the particular knowledge itself.

Hegemony is created and recreated by the formal corpus of school knowledge, as well as by the covert teaching that has gone on and does go on in schools. What on the surface appears to be neutral and unbiased pedagogy really masks the interest of the dominant class while inviting the consent of the dominated (Bourdieu and Passeron, 1977; MacLeod, 1987). What was at first an ideology in the form of class interest has now become the definition of the situation in most school curricula (Apple, 1990). The school needs to make all of this seem natural. A society based on technical cultural capital and individual accumulation of economic capital needs to seem as if it is the only possible world. This requires that institutions, commonsense rules, and knowledge be seen as preordained, neutral, and basically unchanging because they all continue to exist by "consensus" (Gramsci, 1971).

In opposition to the dominant hegemony that proliferates in schools, critical educators argue for the insertion of conflict and debate into the school curriculum. Hegemony is based largely on trust, and conflict among groups is viewed as something that is bad and that should be eliminated from the school environment. Loewen (1995), for instance, argues that the revising of history has negative implications for the politicizing of students and the performance of students from marginalized cultures. It is imperative that urban and working-class students develop positive perspectives toward conflict and change; perspectives that will enable them to deal with the complex and often repressive political realities and the current institutional modes of interaction.

Apple (1990) points to science and social studies as the most explicit examples of hidden teaching. Science, in U.S. schools, is tacitly linked with accepted standards of validity and is seen (and taught) as always subject to empirical verification with no outside influences, either personal or political. Apple critiques this view of science as ignoring the raging debates between competing scientific theories and the occasional conceptual revolutions (or paradigm shifts) that propel the field forward. With respect to social studies, he argues that comparative studies of revolutions and the use of conflict in the legal and economic rights movements of marginalized groups would assist in the formation of a perspective that sees these and similar activities as legitimate models of action. In a similar vein, Loewen (1995) argues that history has been taught to schoolchildren in a manner that encourages patriotism and downplays any wrongdoing by America's leaders, as well as downplaying any cultural conflict or revolutionary activity that may have existed in the history of the Americas. Issues such as conquest, racism, domination, and oppression are often omitted, especially when U.S. citizens are to blame for these actions. History textbooks induce students to believe that history consists of facts to be learned. History is seen as not open to debate. Classes are not encouraged to interrogate history or question the motives of historical actors, nor are they taught to look for bias or accounts alternative to those mentioned in the texts. As Loewen

(1995) notes, "Perhaps adults' biggest reason for lying is that they fear our history—fear that it isn't so wonderful, and that if children were to learn what has really gone on, they would lose all respect for our society" (296). This approach to history, Loewen argues, has damaging consequences.

1. It makes class boring and turns students off.
2. It hurts children's self-image to swallow what their history books teach about the fairness of America, especially Black and Latino children.
3. It leads to decreased motivation and relevance, which, in turn, lead to poorer performance among blacks, other ethnic groups, and women.
4. It encourages the already powerless to be passive learners and hold alliegance to a country that has wronged them.

Critical Pedagogies

Critical pedagogists, in response to social and critical educational theory, examine schools both in their historical context and as part of the existing social and political fabric that characterizes the dominant society (McLaren, 1989). Critical pedagogists also draw inspiration from the work of the Frankfurt School of Critical Theory. Although differences exist, these pedagogists are united in their objectives to empower the marginalized and transform existing social inequalities and injustices. A major task of critical pedagogy has been to disclose and challenge the role schools play in political and cultural life. Especially within the last decade, critical pedagogists have come to view schooling as a highly political and cultural enterprise.

McLaren (1989) asserts pedagogy is simultaneously concerned with the details of what students and others might do together and the cultural politics such practices support. Critical educational theorists, he claims, have responded to the New Right by arguing that the increasing adoption of management-type pedagogies and accountability schemes to meet the logic of market demands has resulted in policy proposals that actively promote the de-skilling of teachers. Critical educational theorists (Aronowitz and Giroux, 1991; Freire, 1997; McLaren, 1989) stress that any genuine pedagogical practice demands a commitment to social transformation in solidarity with subordinated and marginalized groups. Critical pedagogies, then, challenge the assumption that schools, as they are currently situated, function as major sites of social and economic mobility. Proponents of these pedagogies suggest that schooling must be analyzed as a cultural and historical process in which select groups are positioned within asymmetrical relations of power on the basis of specific race, class, and gender groupings.

Critical pedagogies can provide teachers and researchers with a better means of understanding the role that schools actually play within a race-, class-, and gender-divided society. In this effort, theorists have generated categories or concepts for questioning student experiences, texts, teacher ideologies, and aspects of school policy that conservative and liberal analyses too often leave unexplored.

Further, critical pedagogists (Freire, 1970; Giroux, 1997; hooks, 1994; Shor, 1992) would like to pry theories away from academics and incorporate them in educational practice. "They throw down the gauntlet to those conservative and corporate multiculturalists, who wish schools simply to teach students about America's great cultural heritage" (McLaren, 1989). They set out to "relativize" schools as normalizing agencies, as agencies that essentially legitimate existing social relations and practices rendering them normal and natural by dismantling and rearranging the artificial rules and codes that make up classroom reality (McLaren, 1989).

An important mentor to McLaren and many of the critical pedagogists in the United States was the great Brazilian educator Paulo Freire. Freire (1970) juxtaposes the "banking" metaphor for education against his recommended problem-posing education. Freire identifies several characteristics of banking education: the teacher teaches and the students are taught, the teacher knows everything and the student knows nothing, the teacher talks and the students listen, and so on. The interests of the oppressors lie in changing the consciousness of the oppressed, not the situation which oppresses them. For the more the oppressed can be led to adapt to their situation, the more they can be dominated. The solution is not to integrate them into the structure of oppression, but to transform that structure so that they can become beings for themselves. In problem-posing education, through dialogue the teachers and students negotiate the process of learning in the classroom around solving problems that exist. The role of the problem-posing educator is to create, together with the students, the conditions under which knowledge becomes *logos* rather than *doxa*. Problem-posing theory and practice take the people's historicity—that is, the cultural histories of marginalized people—as a starting point.

Lankshear, Peters, and Knobel (1997) project postmodern practices of critical pedagogy into cyberspace and consider the viability of critical pedagogy within an environment where a range of new technologies and practices have converged to produce a communications revolution. These authors argue that critical pedagogy is a viable enterprise within cyberspace. Lankshear, Peters, and Knobel outline the tenets of critical pedagogy as it was defined in modernist spaces, before critiquing some of the contradictions or limitations that resulted from this.

(i) Critical pedagogy in modernist spaces remained strongly teacher-controlled.
(ii) Practices of critical pedagogy within formal settings remained bounded by curriculum and syllabus demands, and failed to account for multiple, contradictory, overlapping social positions.

These problems, Lankshear, Peters, and Knobel argue, originate in spaces of enclosure that characterize the modernist institution of school education. The book, the classroom, and the curriculum can be viewed as intermeshed fixed enclosures.

Practicing critical pedagogy in cyberspace, Lankshear, Peters, and Knobel argue, can force educators to take into account sophisticated notions of multiplicity. Cyberspace calls into question the stability and coherence of the book and the forms of narration enacted upon it. The distinction between the reader and the writer disappears as the reader can add, delete, edit, and modify the text in many ways making the reader the manifest creator of meaning. Also, the social spaces of cyberspace enable subjects to re-examine, play and experiment with, and ultimately transform their own multiplicity (Lankshear, Peters and Knobel, 1997, p. 161). Cyber "space" allows for more democratization, as it is constituted by a logic that is both participatory in nature and interactive in format. Electronically mediated communication tends to break down spaces of institutional enclosure and subvert their mystification of the word-world relation. The radical interactiveness and convertibility of digital text(s) undermine at the level of lived textual practice the very notion of a static, immutable, transcendent reality pictured by the book.

When looking at the potential for critical pedagogy in cyberspace, Lankshear, Knobel, and Peters point to the possibility of digital text exploding the notion that meaning is encased within texts. They also envision digital texts as possibly creating safe places for learners to develop and discover commonalities across difference, and establishing a more egalitarian relationship between students and teachers. In the cyber-world the students may actually have expertise in the technology though teachers remain experts at maintaining an ethos of interrogation and assisting students in conceptualizing and framing their questions and ideas. My work with the students in the Pacific Beach Project attempted to make ample use of cyberspace as an arena of mutual engagement for many of these reasons.

Shor (1992) combines the insights of critical educational theorists such as Freire, Giroux, and Dewey with Piaget's theories of learning and development, which advocate a reciprocal relationship between teacher and student (as opposed to teachers merely transferring knowledge to students via lecture), to analyze the impact of critical pedagogy and empowering education on classroom practices. Empowering education, as Shor defines it, is a critical-democratic pedagogy for self and social change. It is a student-centered program for multicultural democracy in school and society. It approaches individual growth as an active, cooperative, and social process, because the self and society create each other. Teaching, according to Shor, is not a neutral act. A curriculum that avoids questioning school and society is not, as is commonly supposed, politically neutral. It cuts off the students' development as critical thinkers about their world. According to Shor, there are eight values of empowering education: participatory, affective, situated, problem-posing, multicultural, dialogic, desocializing, and democratic learning. In his analysis Shor employs the use of teaching vignettes of K-12 and university settings, covering subjects ranging from literature to science, to illustrate how empowering education can look in various contexts.

Shor's book, *Empowering Education,* provides an explicit critique of what Shor terms traditional education: it suppresses developing skills and intellectual interests; it relegates students to positions of powerlessness, setting them up to accept powerlessness as adults; it fails to acknowledge the strengths, cultures, and prior knowledge of the students; and it gives teachers the ultimate authority. Traditional education encourages disconnection and alienation from the curriculum and schooling. It promotes failure for a large segment of the population, facilitates cultural and social reproduction, and doesn't accurately measure cognitive skills. Shor's work also points to the difficulties that emergent critical educators may face, provides strategies for dealing with these challenges, and advocates for empowering educators to become classroom researchers as well.

It is important to acknowledge that critical pedagogy has at least as many critics as proponents in the educational community. From the conservative right to self-proclaimed radicals, critical pedagogists have been derided for being overly idealistic and theoretical (Ravitch, 2000) or for promoting pedagogy that de-emphasized the role of the educator in imparting important skills that the poor and students of color must learn if they are to be successful in K-12 and postsecondary education. Delpit (1987, 1988, and 1995) claims that it is racist to not teach students of color the skills that they need to get into and succeed in college. She critiques "open and progressive" education that does not teach students how to write a sentence. Delpit recalls her early years as a teacher in Philadelphia during the early 1970s. Her attempts to employ a student-empowering pedagogy led her students to continually lag behind their white and wealthy counterparts attending school in the suburbs. Her students did not improve until she decided to teach them the specific skills that they needed to access and navigate the culture of power. From her research, Delpit has surmised that many progressive white educators think that they are freeing students of color from a racist educational system by allowing them to express themselves without learning to read, write, or speak Standard English. Delpit argues that students will not be able to enter the mainstream of society without these skills.

Delpit's comments must be taken seriously by any educators who plan to use critical theory to engage urban youth. We must resist the urge to focus only on the emergence of critical consciousness without finding ways to link this consciousness to the development of academic skills. For this reason, my study has focused on academic and critical literacies simultaneously in an attempt to link critical consciousness with academic skill development.

It is also important, however, to be critical of stances that are uncritical of the existence of schools as mechanisms of social reproduction. Teaching poor urban students of color to think, act, and speak like wealthy, suburban, white students is not going to ensure their success. Also, an uncritical approach could be dangerous to students' sense of self to the extent that it is uncritical of the status quo in education and fails to make explicit the hegemonic function of schooling. Such critical discourse, however, should seek to transform identities and empower previously oppressed students as it seeks to promote critical reading and writing skills. Further, critical educators should work to create curricula that illuminate the culture of power while also honoring the tradition of cultural studies, which seeks to represent those cultures that have been marginalized by the culture of power.

Cultural Studies and Popular Culture

Giroux (1996) addresses the crisis confronting youth (whom he labels a generation under siege) where they are enmeshed in a *culture of violence* coded by race and class. He speaks to the negative connotations of youth culture promoted in popular media that propel youth toward mistrust, alienation, misogyny, violence, apathy, and the development of *fugitive cultures*. This same media has commercialized the working-class body and criminalized black youth. Critical pedagogists, Giroux argues, must consider popular film and music as serious sites for social knowledge to be discussed, interrogated, and critiqued. While the power in such messages can be used for good or ill, few can dispute the impact of popular culture in the lives of urban working-class youth. Giroux promotes a synthesis of critical pedagogy and cultural studies to gain a critical understanding of how youth are being constructed differently within a popular culture that is simultaneously oppressive and resistant and represents violence as a legitimate practice to define youth identity. In making a case for using cultural studies as the conceptual frame for analyzing the contemporary problems of youth, Giroux states:

> Cultural studies, with its ambiguous founding moments spread across multiple continents and diverse institutional spheres, has always been critically attentive to the changing conditions influencing the socialization of youth and the social and economic contexts producing such changes. The self and social formation of diverse youth subcultures mediated by popular cultural forms remain prominent concerns of cultural studies. (1996, p. 15)

Cultural studies offers educators a language through which to analyze and critique, yet it is incomplete without critical pedagogy as a mode of cultural criticism and social action. Educators, says Giroux (1996), must become public intellectuals who adeptly employ this language of critique combined with a questioning pedagogy to help youth make sense of the dangerous and damaging messages sent to them through popular media.

Cultural studies focuses on contemporary culture from nonelite or counterhegemonic perspectives "from below," with an openness to the culture's reception and production in everyday life, or, more generally, its impact on life trajectories. It encourages and takes notice of culture's capacity to express and invoke less restricted ("other," counter-normative) ways of living. Engaged cultural studies aims to produce knowledge from perspectives lost to the dominant public culture and to listen to far-off or marginalized voices. As a field, cultural studies accepts that studying culture is rarely value-free, and so, embracing clearly articulated, progressive antiracist, antisexist, anticolonial and anti-neoliberal values, it seeks to extend and critique the relatively narrow range of norms, methods, and practices embedded in the traditional, past-fixated, canon-forming humanities (During, 1999).

As an anti-discipline (Hall, 1999), cultural studies is not wedded to any one methodological approach. Rather, it encompasses multiple avenues for investigating and documenting the complex relationships between ideology, culture, language, and power in late capitalist societies. Cultural studies, however, does lean toward anthropological methods, such as the critical ethnographic method that the present study employs. As During (1999) writes, regarding the relationship between cultural studies and critical ethnography:

> As we have begun to see, the discipline's turn to ethnography in particular was motivated by the desire to move beyond theoretical discourses which, however insightful, have been restricted to higher education institutions. Ethnography . . .was important to cultural studies because it provided a method by which the discipline could escape such restrictions, and it remains crucial to an understanding of the current and future directions of the discipline. Cultural studies ethnography, particularly of media audiences, has mainly used qualitative research in order to avoid the pitfalls of sociological objectivity and functionalism and to give room to voices other than the theorist's own. For cultural studies, knowledge based on statistical techniques belongs to the processes that "normalize" society and stand in opposition to cultural studies' respect for the marginal subject. (pp. 17–18)

Cultural theorists analyze the social and political context within which culture manifests itself. Its founders, British intellectuals who had emerged from the working class, intended cultural studies to be both an intellectual and a pragmatic enterprise (praxis) committed to a moral evaluation of modern society and to a radical line of political action (Hall, 1998; Sardar and Van Loon, 1998). Cultural studies aims to understand and change the structures of dominance everywhere, but in industrial capitalist societies in particular. Cultural studies employs the field of semiotics as a conceptual frame for understanding issues such as the representation of the Other. The most common representation of the Other is as the darker side, the binary opposite of oneself. We are civilized; they are barbaric. The colonists are hard working; the natives are lazy. Heterosexuals are moral and good; homosexuals are immoral and evil (During, 1999; Sardar and Van Loon, 1998). Skin color and phenotypes can be construed by the dominant society as signs (signifiers) and the media and the educational system can help determine the signified meaning.

Cultural studies criticizes multiculturalism for solely taking race into account when discussing identity. According to theorists, multiculturalism has tended to reproduce the "saris, samosas, and steel bands syndrome" (Sardar and Van Loon, 1998); that is, it focuses on superficial manifestations of culture and makes them exotic. It views different cultures in terms of how "different" they are from English culture, not on their own terms. Theorists argue that identities are constituted by power relations. Western representations of race have created ethnic identities through novels, theater, painting, film, and so on. Ethnic identity is thus largely a social construct that divides various cultural groups into "imagined communities" by bonding them together in literary and visual narrations located in territory, history, and memory.

Williams (1995) offers a historical analysis of the social organization of culture in terms of its institutions and formations. Williams asserts that the term "sociology of culture" implies a convergence of various interests and methods. His sociology of culture has helped to evolve the discourse from the notion of a restricted high culture to a notion of culture as ordinary, as a way of life or structure of feeling lived and experienced by the vast majority of people in a given society. This conception is important because it implies that all people have culture, not only those who belong to the dominant elite. It is also important for critical educators who want to deconstruct hegemonic curricula that attempt to infuse "culture" into so called a-cultural or culturally deprived urban youth. Finally, Williams's analysis supports the serious intellectual study of the everyday experiences of marginalized urban youth.

Williams (1995) sees the emergence of a general human culture in specific societies where it is shaped by local and temporary systems. He examines language in all of the forms in which it has been used to give meaning to lived experience. He also argues that there is no such thing as the masses, only ways of seeing people as masses. Mass or ordinary culture is not implicitly good or bad, but the practice of assigning value can be tied to existing ideological structures that hold ordinary people, their efforts, and their artifacts in contempt.

Williams (1995) demonstrates that the concept of culture came into existence as a holistic protest against the fragmenting effects of industrialism, and he strongly suggests that both "ordinary" culture and "the best that has been known and thought," therefore, belong to a common heritage of opposition. He employs popular culture as an example of a generally oppositional cultural form that can be produced in and by, rather than outside and against, capitalist consumerism. He further suggests that the sociology of culture be used to blur the lines between the cultural critic and the military/industrial technician, and he shows how critics must work from within the systems that they define themselves against.

Williams looks forward to the birth of a new, major discipline that will deal with culture very differently, and he begins to lay the theoretical groundwork for cultural studies. He makes several recommendations for a sociology of culture.

1. It must concern itself with the social processes of all cultural production, including the forms of production, which can be designated as ideologies.
2. It must concern itself with the institutions and formations of cultural production.
3. It must concern itself with the social relations of its specific means of production.
4. It must concern itself with specific artistic forms.
5. It must concern itself with the processes of social and cultural reproduction.
6. It must concern itself with general and specific problems of cultural organization.

Williams and other scholars at the Birmingham Centre for Contemporary Cultural Studies (CCCS) helped lay the theoretical groundwork for the study of popular culture as both a product of the capitalist economy and a site for counterhegemonic resistance. Many of the early cultural theorists (Adorno and Horkheimer, 1999) saw popular culture as merely a tool of the culture industry. The postmodern influence on cultural studies, with its critiques of meta-narratives (even leftist, neo-Marxist ones) and its honoring of multiple perspectives, however, created the space for alternate conceptions of the role of popular cultures in a capitalist order. Turning from its original attack on mass culture, many within the discipline began to celebrate aspects of commercial culture—cultural populism—arguing that some cultural products have quasi-political effects, independent of education and critical discourse. It is important, however, not to overlook the power of co-optation. During (1999) argues that cultural populism requires a highly nuanced account of the relations between cultural markets and cultural products, in order convincingly to celebrate (some) popular culture as progressive. Those who choose to study popular culture must be conscious of both its relationship to and its critique of dominant ideologies and dominant markets. In my own work, which exposes urban youth to the critical research of popular culture, I constantly strive to keep the duality of cultural products central to the discourse and analyses.

Docker (1994), however, questions the way a century of modernist critical theory has made sense of twentieth-century mass culture and suggests that postmodernism may promise more illuminating approaches. Modernism, he feels, has demonized mass culture as the chief danger to civilization. Postmodernism, on the other hand, does not ascribe to popular culture phenomena any single commanding meaning or purpose (in other words, it does not present a grand narrative of popular culture and its "impact" on society). It does not assume any easily explicable relationship between popular culture and its audiences, and it does not see audiences as transparent in their desires and consciousness. Also, it does not see a hierarchy or genres in culture in general. Instead, postmodernism is interested in a plurality of forms and genres, a pluralizing of aesthetic criteria, and a respect for the interacting, conflicting, and contested histories of these genres. Postmodernism sees popular culture as a frequent site of flamboyance, extravagance, excess, parody, self-parody, and sometimes even resistance.

Storey's (1998) work illuminates many of Docker's ideas and offers a set of concrete definitions for popular culture. He asserts that popular culture is always defined implicitly or explicitly, in contrast to other conceptual categories such as folk culture, mass culture, or dominant culture, and he argues the following.

1. Popular culture is culture that is well liked by many people.
2. Popular culture is what is left over after we have decided what is high culture (the notion of popular culture as substandard culture).
3. Popular culture is mass culture.
4. Popular culture is that culture which originates from the people.
5. Popular culture is a neo-Gramscian concept. (1998, pp. 6–13).

Hegemony for Gramsci is a cultural concept developed to explain the absence of socialist revolutions in Western capitalist democracies. The concept of hegemony is used by Gramsci to refer to a condition or process in which a dominant class not merely rules a society, but leads it through the exercise of moral and intellectual leadership. In this sense, the concept is used to suggest a society in which, despite oppression and exploitation, there is a high degree of consensus and a large measure of social stability; a society in which the subordinate groups and classes appear to support meanings that bind them to, and incorporate them into, the prevailing structures of power. In this last approach, popular culture is seen as a site of struggle between the forces of resistance of subordinate groups in society, and the forces of incorporation of dominant groups in society. Popular culture in this usage is not an imposed mass culture, or a people's culture; it is more of a terrain of exchange between the two. The texts and practices of popular culture move within what Gramsci (1971) calls a compromise equilibrium. Those who look at popular culture from a neo-Gramscian perspective tend to see it as a terrain of ideological struggle between dominant and subordinate classes, or dominant and subordinate cultures.

Using a neo-Gramscian analysis, popular culture can be viewed as the cultural products created by men and women as they make sense of their active consumption of the texts and practices of the culture industries. Youth cultures, for example, are able to appropriate for their own purposes and meanings the commodities that are commercially provided. For instance, in popular musical genres such as reggae and hip-hop, it is possible to have anticapitalist politics articulated in the economic interests of capitalism. The music may be lubricating the very system that it seeks to condemn (Lipsitz, 1994). It may exist as an expression of oppositional politics that produces political and cultural effects in a form that is of financial benefit to the dominant culture. Storey (1998) argues that cultural theorists must be aware of the simultaneous possibilities of the making of popular culture for subordinate groups. It has the potential of empowerment and resistance, but it can also lead to passivity and consumption of the hegemonic ideals promoted by the traditional intellectuals of the dominant class.

In *Postmodernism and Education,* Aronowitz and Giroux (1991) argue that the curriculum can best inspire learning only when school knowledge builds upon the tacit knowledge derived from the cultural resources that students already possess. For example, electronically mediated popular culture, which, it can be shown, is produced from a constellation of influences of which black speech is a crucial element, is treated by postmodern education as a legitimate object of knowledge.

For postmodern education it is not a question of substituting popular culture for traditional high-culture topics. Instead, the traditional curriculum must meet the test of relevance to a student-centered learning regime where "relevance" is not coded as the rejection of tradition but is a criterion for determining inclusion. It is the task of the teacher to persuade students that knowledges contribute to helping them learn what they need to know. In any case, the canons are no longer taught as self-evident repositories of enlightenment. Rather, the teacher is obliged to encourage students to interrogate the values underlying a work of literature. Educators are forced to rethink the nature of legitimate knowledge.

Postmodern education deconstructs the canon. Aronowitz and Giroux (1991) also write in response to the conservative educational politics of the Reagan-Bush era as professed through the work of such scholars as Bloom and Hirsch. This conservative attack endeavored to provide a programmatic language with which to defend schools as cultural sites, that is, as institutions responsible for reproducing the knowledge and values necessary to advance the historical values of Western culture. Bloom (1988) proposed a series of education reforms that privileged a fixed idea of Western culture organized around a core curriculum based on the old "Great Books." For Bloom, popular culture and, in particular, rock music, represents a new form of barbarism. Hirsch (1987) argues for a view of cultural literacy that serves both as a critique of many existing theories of education and as a referent for a reconstructed vision of American public schooling that is cleansed of its critical and emancipatory possibilities.

Many prominent educational theorists (Carnoy and Levin, 1985; Dewey, 1916; Bowles and Gintis, 1976; Goodlad, 1984) have shared faith in the modernist ideals that stress the capacity of individuals to think critically, to exercise social responsibility, and to remake the world in the interest of the Enlightenment dream of reason and freedom. Aronowitz and Giroux (1991), however, argue that the challenge of postmodernism is important for educators because it raises crucial questions regarding hegemonic aspects of modernism and, by implication, how these have affected the meaning and dynamics of present-day schooling.

Postmodernist criticism is also important because it offers the promise of deterritorializing modernism and redrawing its political, social, and cultural boundaries, while simultaneously affirming a politics of racial, gender, and ethnic difference. Moreover, postmodern criticism does not merely challenge dominant Western cultural models with their attendant notion of universally valid knowledge; it also resituates us within a world that bears little resemblance to the one that inspired the grand narratives of Marx and Freud. In effect, postmodern criticism calls attention to the shifting boundaries related to the increasing influence of the electronic mass media and information technology, the changing nature of class and social formations in postindustrialized capitalist societies, and the growing transgression of boundaries between life and art, high and popular culture, and image and reality.

The postmodern condition is also rooted in the fundamental political and technological shifts that undermine the central modernist notion that there exists a legitimate center; a unique and superior position from which to establish control and determine hierarchies. This center refers to the privileging of Western patriarchal culture. Related to the critique of master narratives and theories of totality is another major concern of postmodernism: the development of a politics that addresses popular culture as a serious object of aesthetic and cultural criticism, on the one hand, and signals and affirms the importance of minority cultures as historically specific forms of cultural production, on the other.

Curriculum theory and specifically the English curriculum, is sorely in need of a theory of textual authority that allows teachers and students to understand how both knowledge and classroom social relations are constructed in ways that may either silence or empower. Textual authority, in this approach, is developed as part of a wider analysis of the struggle over culture fought out at the levels of curriculum knowledge, pedagogy, and the exercise of institutional power. In addition, postmodern educationists argue for the necessity of developing a politics and pedagogy of voice as part of a theory of curriculum that opens up texts to a wider range of meanings and interpretations, while simultaneously constructing student experience as part of a broader discourse of critical citizenship and democracy. Interrogating the connection between language and power is crucial for understanding how educational workers might view curriculum theory as a form of textual authority that legitimates a particular form of discursive practice. Understanding curriculum as a part of a broader struggle between dominant and subordinate discourses has critical implications for the ways in which educators produce and "read" curriculum, engage the notion of student experience, and critically redefine their own role as engaged public intellectuals. Literature of the Other provides all students with the opportunity to identify, unravel, and critically debate the codes, vocabularies, and ideologies of various cultural traditions.

Following several tendencies in critical and social theory, some theorists claim that the foundations of legitimate knowledge have collapsed. There are new, socially constructed objects of knowledge and new ways of seeing them that radically transgress disciplinary boundaries. But the new paradigm of social and cultural knowledge also challenges the Enlightenment conception that knowledge can be constructed on irrefutable foundations that are the irreducible starting point of inquiry, as well as on older methods by which this knowledge may be adduced. Postmodernism interrogates the privileged space of high art in the panoply of aesthetic discourses. Cultural studies, postmodernists argue, investigates the degree to which what is privileged in art may be historically and conventionally prescribed.

Aronowitz and Giroux (1991) argue that, since it is no longer possible to stand on the foundations of past savants, the canon that derives from these foundations must be interrogated. New intellectuals who refuse to preserve the tradition as a basis for shaping the future, but instead argue in favor of a new skepticism or in another register propose a counter-canon consisting of marginal discourses. Critical postmodernism insists that the products of the so-called mass culture, popular and folk art forms, are proper objects of study, not, as some modernist film criticism argues, to establish their aesthetic credentials, but to challenge aesthetics itself as a legitimate discourse of exclusion.

Any viable educational theory, postmodernists argue, has to begin with a language that links schooling to democratic public life, defines teachers as engaged intellectuals and border crossers, and develops forms of pedagogy that incorporate difference, plurality, and the language of the everyday as central to the production and legitimization of learning. But this demands the reconstruction of a view of language and theory that establishes the groundwork for viewing schooling and education as a form of cultural politics, as a discourse that draws its meaning from the social, cultural, and economic context in which it operates. For further discussion of viable educational theories that reconsider the relationships between language, discourse, culture, and power in capitalist societies, I turn to new literacy studies. This growing field of literacy research also sheds light on the role that the critical study of popular cultures can play in creating new literacies that uncover and challenge these traditional relationships.

New Literacy Studies and Popular Culture

What are the new literacy studies? Why do they provide an important framework for understanding how the study and incorporation of popular culture can be empowering academically and critically to diverse members of marginalized groups? New literacy theorists (Ferdman, 1990; Heath, 1983; Mahiri, 1998; Pattison, 1982; Street, 1993) critique autonomous models of literacy (Goody and Watt, 1968; Olson, 1977; Ong, 1982) that seek out the cognitive consequences of literacy and they offer alternative, "ideological" models that incorporate social and cultural contexts as well as the power relations implicit in literacy practices. New literacy studies offer more anthropological and cross-cultural frameworks to replace those of a previous era, in which psychological and culturally narrow approaches predominated. Research in cultures that have newly acquired reading and writing draws our attention to cultural concerns and interests. Research into vernacular literacies within modern settings has begun to show the richness and diversity of literacy practices and meanings despite the pressures for uniformity exerted by the nation state and the modern education systems.

Street (1993) discusses the ideological model of literacy that will enable new literacy theorists to focus on the ways in which the apparent neutrality of literacy practices disguises their significance for the distribution of power in society and for power relations. Just as research relating to popular culture indicates, Street suggests that it is at the interface between sociolinguistic and anthropological theories, on the one hand, and between discourse and ethnographic method on the other, that future research in the field of literacy studies will be conducted. Street provides an explicit critique of the autonomous model of literacy that conceptualizes literacy in technical terms, treating it as independent of social context, an autonomous variable whose consequences for society can be derived from its intrinsic character. Researchers dissatisfied with the autonomous model of literacy and with the assumptions outlined above have come to view literacy practices as inextricably linked to cultural and power structures in society and to recognize the variety of cultural practices associated with reading and writing in different contexts. A number of researchers in the new literacy studies have also paid greater attention to the role of literacy practices in reproducing or challenging structures of power and domination. Street uses the term "ideological" to describe this new approach to literacy studies because it signals quite explicitly that literacy practices are aspects not only of culture but also of power structures. The very emphasis on the neutrality and autonomy of literacy is itself ideological in the sense of disguising this power dimension.

Literacy, Street (1993) claims, can no longer be addressed as a neutral technology as in the reductionist autonomous model; it is already a social and ideological practice involving fundamental aspects of epistemology, power, and politics. The acquisition of literacy involves challenges to dominant discourses, shifts in what constitutes the agenda of proper literacy, and struggles for power and position. In this sense, then, literacy practices are saturated with ideology. The ideological model does not attempt to deny the technical skill or the cognitive aspects of reading and writing, but rather understands them as they are encapsulated within cultural wholes and structures of power. In this sense the ideological model subsumes rather than excludes the work undertaken within the autonomous model. The autonomous model of literacy had generated two main strands of inquiry, one concerned with questions about the consequences of reading and writing for individual and cognitive processes, the other considering the functional operation of literacy within specific modern institutions. Neither approach paid sufficient attention to the social and ideological character of literacy.

Street also speaks to the importance of paying attention to the wider parameters of (social and cultural) context when analyzing discourse or the relationship between orality and literacy. He points to the need to situate the ideological model within a firm theoretical grounding such as those provided by the ethnographic method and social anthropology.

"We are inadequately literate," Pattison (1982) argues, "in part because we have inadequate ideas about literacy." Pattison seeks to improve our literacy by defining the term accurately. He sets out to debunk certain premises concerning literacy such as the following: literacy is equivalent to reading and writing; individuals who can read and write are more cultured than those who are not; and reading and writing should be propagated among poor people as a first step in their economic and social development. Instead, Pattison offers that literacy is above all consciousness of the problems posed by language and only secondarily skill in the technologies by which this consciousness is expressed. Further, he suggests that literacy is culturally defined and there can be no universal standard of literacy.

Pattison also believes that the imposition of narrow Western ideas about literacy on developing populations is not automatically beneficial and that literacy changes in step with changing notions about language and with new technologies. Pattison defines literacy as consciousness of the questions posed by language coupled with mastery of the skills by which a culture at any given moment in its history manifests this consciousness. Literacy, he argues, is always tied to power and access. With respect to reading and writing, Pattison goes to great lengths to demonstrate that these technologies of language are not, in and of themselves, directly associated with literacy, as many literacy theorists had previously suggested (Goody and Watt [1968] attempted to theorize a "Great Divide" between oral and "literate" cultures).

Pattison (1982) provides a historical overview of the relationship between speech and writing in an attempt to debunk simplistic notions of a dualistic hierarchy. He offers critiques by scholars from oral cultures on the negative consequences of writing and claims that there can be no assurance that a world where everyone reads and writes will be a better world. In offering the example of

Homer's *Odyssey*, a relic of the oral age, Pattison argues that people who know their culture by oral transmission may yet think as critical individuals while those who have been reared on the written text may still act like sheep. Writing, in fact, has often been used as a tool of authoritarianism as Pattison suggests, offering the example of how the Christian Church controlled written literacy and access to the language of power in the West for centuries. In his discussion of the advent of print, Pattison speaks of the relationship between notions of literacy and technological advancement as he opens the space for an emerging electronic literacy (or literacies) that will be at least as closely connected to power and access as print literacy.

Finally, Pattison makes an important distinction between what he calls *functional* or *mechanical literacy* and *critical literacy*. Depending on their expected station in life, children are either taught to merely be functional (subordinates) or critical (elites). Hull (1993) defines critical literacy as not only learning to decode or inscribe texts, but learning to assess those texts, to read their world in an attempt to understand the relations of power and domination that underlie and inform and create them, and ultimately act to change them.

Pattison advocates for the elevation of a *popular literacy* that is keyed into the spoken language and culture of the people. This new literacy, operated through the electronic media, can create a new space for critical thought that can displace the preeminence of the middle-class literacy approved by the American establishment. Youth and the poor can be invigorated by an acknowledgment of the literacy that speaks to their experience and, in turn, struggle to create a more democratic existence. Pattison's concept of popular literacy is quite compatible with critical, cultural, and sociocultural approaches, which would argue that any meaningful literacy learning must start with the cultural practices of the people. Following Williams's social definition of culture, Pattison equates these cultural practices with the everyday experiences of ordinary people.

Ferdman (1990) also argues that cultural diversity has significant implications for the processes of becoming and being literate. Utilizing a social-psychological perspective, he explores the relationship between literacy and the way in which a person's identity as a member of an ethnocultural group (cultural identity) is intertwined with the meaning and consequences of becoming and being literate. Ferdman asserts that literacy is culturally framed and defined and, as a result, members of different cultures will differ in what they view as literate behavior. This can influence how individuals engage in literacy acquisition and activity. The current diversity in educational achievement and scholastic literacy development among ethnic groups is a tragic consequence of our lack of attention to this relationship. Ferdman concludes that the connections between literacy and culture must be fully acknowledged and better understood in order to achieve the goal of literacy acquisition for all.

Freire and Macedo (1987) offer a radical view of literacy (radical pedagogy) that revolves around the importance of naming and transforming the ideological and social conditions that undermine the possibility for forms of community and public life organized around the imperatives of a critical democracy. An *emancipatory theory of literacy* points to the need to develop an alternative discourse and critical reading of how ideology, culture, and power work within the late capitalist societies to limit, disorganize, and marginalize the more critical and radical everyday experiences and commonsense perceptions of individuals. Literacy, for Freire, is part of the process of becoming self-critical about the historically constructed nature of one's experience. To be able to name one's experience is part of what it means to "read" the world and to begin to understand the political nature of the limits and possibilities that make up the larger society. To be literate is not to be free; it is to be present and active in the struggle to reclaim one's voice, history, and future. As part of the discourse of narrative and agency, critical literacy suggests using history as a form of liberating memory. History means recognizing the figural traces of untapped potentialities as well as the sources of suffering that constitute one's past. Freire and Macedo (1987) assert that a radical theory of literacy needs to be constructed around a dialectical theory of voice and empowerment:

> Reading the world, the true aim of critical literacy, always precedes reading the word, and reading the word implies continually reading the world. Reading the word is not merely preceded by reading the world, but by a certain form of writing it or rewriting it, that is, of transforming it by means of conscious, practical work. Words should be laden with the meaning of the people's existential experience, and not of the teacher's experience. A critical reading of reality constitutes an act of what Gramsci calls counterhegemony. (p. 35)

Freire and Macedo's (1987) work also discusses the relationship between literacy and pedagogy. A radical pedagogy, centered upon critical and liberating dialogue, helps to impart critical literacy to oppressed people. When challenged by a critical educator, students begin to understand that the more profound dimension of their freedom lies exactly in the recognition of constraints that can be overcome. They can discover for themselves in the process of becoming more and more critical that it is impossible to deny the constitutive power of their consciousness in the social practice in which they participate. A radical pedagogy is dialectical and aims to enable students to become critical of the hegemonic practices that have shaped their experiences and perceptions in the hope of freeing themselves from the bonds of these dominating ideologies. In order for this to happen, learners must be involved in transformative discourse, which legitimizes the wishes, decisions, and dreams of the people involved. An example of this is Freire's use of *popular culture notebooks* in Sao Tome and Principe where he created exercise books out of the worlds and experiences of the learners' communities.

Freire and Macedo (1987) argue strongly for the use of the native language as a prerequisite for the development of any literacy campaign that purports to serve as the means to a critical appropriation of one's own culture and history. Educators must fully understand the broad meaning of students' empowerment, which enables students to interrogate and selectively appropriate those aspects of the dominant culture that will provide them with the basis for defining and transforming the wider social order. Students' language must not be viewed as subordinated and antagonistic to the dominant language. Educators must develop literacy programs that move away from traditional approaches that emphasize the acquisition of mechanical skills. The reader's development of a critical comprehension of the text and the sociohistorical context to which it refers becomes an important factor in Freire's notion of literacy.

Heath (1983) championed the use of ethnography as she lived with students and families in the Piedmont Carolinas for ten years looking at the *literacy events* of three communities: Maintown, Roadville, and Trackton. Heath found that the types of literacy events promoted in the cultures of the towns had a profound effect on the ability of students to understand the literacy activities of schools. For instance, middle-class parents in Maintown modeled the question-answer pattern of teachers in schools. The parent knew the response to the question, but both parties understood it to be a game. In Trackton, inhabited largely by working-class African-Americans, the parents would not ask a question to which they knew the answer. Parents purchased few books for their children. Reading was done basically to accomplish daily tasks, or the children read to learn. In Trackton, reading was a public and group affair; its inhabitants placed more emphasis on orality than did the school system, which viewed literacy in narrow terms related strictly to decoding print. This does not mean that the students were unable to read, as Heath documents their ability to decode print as early as age three. Similarly, in Roadville, a white working-class community, reading was promoted rhetorically, but it was mainly viewed as an activity to gain information, to be tolerated rather than enjoyed. Few people read unless they had to. Those who did read hardly acted on anything they had read. The mothers in Roadville read bedtime stories but asked only simple, formulaic questions and had a difficult time keeping the children's attention. Heath concluded her work by encouraging teachers to be ethnographers of students' lives and worlds. Such studies can alert urban teachers to the marginalized popular cultures that permeate the lives of their students.

Gee (1999) argues for a sociocultural perspective on literacy and language learning. He asserts that people do not learn languages at the level of "English" or "Russian"; rather, they learn what he calls "social languages." At the level of social languages, there is no such thing as fixed meaning. Meaning is customized in the here and now as we speak/write or listen/read. Gee (1999) makes a distinction between authentic beginners and false beginners. Authentic beginners are people who have come to learning sites without the early preparation, prealignment in terms of cultural values, and sociocultural resources that more advantaged learners at those sites have. False beginners are those from homes that have given them preparation and cultural alignment. When they enter school, the false beginners look like quick learners, and the authentic beginners are often marginalized even though they may be making substantial progress.

Gee's first claim is that teaching and learning language and literacy is not about teaching and learning "English," but about teaching and learning specific social languages. He then provides an example of a college student, Jane, who shares the same story using two distinct social languages with her boyfriend and her parents. Gee argues that the different social languages allow Jane to make visible and recognizable two different versions of who she is, two different socially situated identities. These socially situated identities are inherently social and relational. The different social languages also allow Jane to make visible and recognizable two different doings, two different socially situated activities. Gee also, through an example from scientific writing, shows that social languages are highly relevant to academic and professional settings.

Gee's second claim is that, in the realm of social languages, there is no meaning. Words, rather, are associated with different "situated" or "customized" meanings in different contexts. A situated meaning is an image or pattern that we assemble on the spot, in context, as we communicate based on our construal of that context and our past experiences. Whatever generality we sense these words to have is due to the fact that words, with their situated meanings, are always associated with or trigger the application of cultural models. Cultural models are "storylines," families of connected images, theories shared by people belonging to specific social or cultural groups. Cultural models are nearly always ideologically laden.

Gee (1999) provides an interaction with a Korean doctoral student as an example of his argument. Although the student spoke fluent English for a Korean citizen, her lack of knowledge of the social languages associated with doctoral studies prevented her from accomplishing anything significant. The Korean student, Gee argues, did not need to learn more English. She needed to learn how to design utterances within a specific form of language so as to trigger a specific identity, specific activities, and specific situated meanings, with their associated cultural models. What the student needed was a mastery of the Discourse. Gee defines a "Discourse" as ways of combining specific social languages with specific ways of acting-interacting-thinking-believing-valuing-feeling as well as ways of coordinating and getting coordinated by other people, tools, technologies, objects, artifacts, and "appropriate" times and places so as to get recognized as enacting a socially situated identity and an appropriately related activity.

Discourses, Gee (1999) claims, are inherently and irredeemably political as is the process of acquiring them. They are political because (1) internal to Discourse there are almost always hierarchical positions; (2) Discourses are partly defined in relationships of alignment and conflict with other Discourses; and (3) Discourses are harder to acquire and tension-filled for authentic beginners. Gee also identifies the necessary conditions for the acquisition of a social language within a discourse such as: situated meanings, cultural models, identities, activities, social languages, and critical framing. Most importantly, Gee contends that authentic beginners must become sociologists and critical theorists of Discourses in general.

Mahiri (1998) contends that teachers can become sources of resistance to the ideology and practices of cultural domination and exploitation that permeate institutional structures in this society, by working to better understand and build on the authentic experiences of students who have been marginalized by the educational process. This can be achieved by the creation of counterhegemonic curricula. This work builds on Street's (1993) and other theories of cultural models of literacy and the methodology of the ethnography of communication to explore the contesting and transcendence of structures of domination which can occur through the negotiation of discourse and print in communicative acts and literacy events. Mahiri draws on findings and implications from several research projects to suggest ways that classroom discourse, curricula, and culture can be changed to enhance processes of teaching and learning by building more powerfully on the authentic experiences of students. These projects include a neighborhood youth basketball league, a freshman college writing program, and a study of the pedagogy of secondary teachers in Northern California and Chicago.

Mahiri looks at African-American culture and youth or popular culture as sites where young people have forged a common identity manifested in dress, language use, music, video games, and common heroes. It is his argument that aspects of popular culture can act as unifying and equalizing forces in culturally diverse classrooms and that African-American and youth cultural sources for curricula can motivate learning of traditional subject matter as well. Mahiri provides a futuristic vision of "new century" schools that promote diversity of culture and perspectives in the classroom, allow for multiple literacies and presentations of knowledge, and utilize technological advances to facilitate literacy development.

Sociocultural Theory: Situated Learning as Legitimate Peripheral Participation within Communities of Practice

Any theory of literacy implies a theory of learning (Barton and Hamilton, 1998). Sociocultural theorists believe that learning as it normally occurs is a function of the activity, context, and culture in which it is situated (Lave and Wenger, 1991). This contrasts with most classroom learning activities which involve knowledge which is abstract and out of context. Social interaction is a critical component of situated learning; learners become involved in a "community of practice" which embodies certain beliefs and behaviors to be acquired (Wenger, 1998).

As beginners or newcomers move from the periphery of this community to its center, they become more active and engaged within the culture and hence assume the role of expert or old-timer. These ideas are what Lave and Wenger (1991) call the process of "legitimate peripheral participation." According to Lave and Wenger:

> Learning viewed as situated activity has as its central defining characteristic a process that we call legitimate peripheral participation. By this we mean to draw attention to the point that learners inevitably participate in communities of practitioners and that mastery of knowledge and skill requires newcomers to move toward full participation in the sociocultural practice of a community. Legitimate peripheral participation provides a way to speak about the relations between newcomers and old-timers, and about activities, identities, artifacts, and communities of knowledge and practice. It concerns the process by which newcomers become part of a community of practice. (1991, p. 29)

Lave and Wenger (1991) outline several principles for legitimate peripheral participation that are central to the focus on literacy development in this study:

- Knowledge needs to be presented in an authentic context; that is, settings and applications that would normally involve that knowledge.
- Learning requires social interaction and collaboration.
- This framework places learning at the intersection of community, shared practice, identity, and meaning.

A community of practice is a site of learning and action in which people come together around a joint enterprise, in the process developing a whole repertoire of activities, common stories, and ways of speaking and acting. Communities of practice constitute reality in a particular manner and encourage specialized ways of acting and thinking (Wenger, 1998).

Communities of practice are social sites where people participate in joint activity as they become certain "kinds of persons." These activities embody distinctive ways in which participants relate to each other and the broader world. Learning occurs constantly in these communities as people participate in activities that are more and more central to the core practice. This changing participation leads participants to take on new identities that are necessarily bound up with new knowledge and skills. Lave (1996) identifies crafting identities as a *social* process and becoming more knowledgeably skilled as an aspect of participation in social practice. By such reasoning, who you are becoming shapes crucially and fundamentally what you "know."

This study seeks to build upon the works of social, critical, cultural, new literacy, and sociocultural theorists. While I acknowledge that there is some merit to the notion of culturally relevant teaching as it is currently articulated, I argue against essentialized notions that treat culture as static and equate it with a socially constructed monoracial identity. By weaving together various theoretical strands, I lay the foundation for a new approach to literacy instruction and literacy learning in urban schools. My approach situates literacy teaching and learning in the everyday experiences of urban youth. This approach to culture as rooted in people's everyday experiences represents a fundamental shift from conceptions of culture as a monoracial identity. Through legitimate peripheral participation in critical research communities of practice that forefront authentic dialogue rooted in urban, youth, and popular cultures, youth are able to take ownership of the research enterprise and transform it, while simultaneously developing intellectual and transformational identities along with academic and critical literacies.

Social theory identifies the hegemonic practices of schools as a key component in the maintenance of the reproduction of inequality. A counterhegemonic curriculum that is centered upon the critical interrogation of popular cultures and contemporary urban issues can prove disruptive to the cycle of social reproduction, as urban youth gain a greater consciousness of the causes of their oppression that are not rooted in deficit theories. As the students' stories and experiences become the curriculum, there is a greater ability to increase literacy learning as students move through a "zone of proximal development" (Vygotsky, 1978) that respects their cultural histories.

Critical pedagogues (Freire, 1970) identify and critique banking notions of education that treat the oppressed as empty objects waiting to receive deposits of knowledge. My approach not only seeks to center dialogue and generativity, but it also employs a sociocultural theory that views learning as changing participation in joint sociocultural activity (Lave and Wenger, 1991).

Finally, my approach to literacy teaching and learning is explicitly critical of discourse that fails to acknowledge the fluidity and multiplicity of culture and the relationship between culture and power in society. A postmodern, cultural studies approach allows space for the discussion and analysis of youth, popular, and urban cultures as simultaneously sites of affinity and resistance that transcend racial identities and sites of commodification and co-optation by the culture industries (Lipsitz 1994; Adorno and Horkheimer, 1999).

All of these theoretical strands are compatible with new literacy studies, which seeks to situate literacy as a social and cultural practice while making explicit the relationship between literacy and power (Barton and Hamilton, 2000; Street, 1993). I bring these perspectives together to analyze the potential impact, on literacy learning, of interventions and projects that allow urban students and teachers to position themselves as critical readers and researchers of popular cultures. This positioning, I argue, creates pedagogic spaces that facilitate the transformative discourse that leads to greater learning and understandings while increasing the development of both academic and critical literacies for diverse, urban student populations.

3

METHOD

Employing a cultural studies epistemology that draws upon critical theory, post-modernism, and Marxism, this critical ethnography was designed to capture and analyze literacy practices and literacy events that demonstrate the development of academic mastery and critical consciousness as urban secondary students move from legitimate peripheral participation toward fuller participation in a critical research community of practice. I chose an epistemological framework that recognized the intricate relationship between culture, class, and power in capitalist society. Such recognition, I believe, is fundamental to a discussion of literacy development amongst marginalized populations. I also situated the study in a paradigm that is explicit about the political and ideological nature of all research and is, therefore, geared toward transformational social action for and with oppressed peoples.

In what follows I explain the rationale for selecting Pacific Beach High School as a focal site and briefly introduce the school (chapter 4 contains a much more thorough introduction to the culture and history of Pacific Beach High). I next introduce the participants in the study and discuss the criteria I used for selecting focal students and focal teachers. Also, I explain my methods of data collection and my strategy for data analysis. I conclude with a brief sketch of my own social location as a researcher and explain how my background has influenced the questions I ask and my methods of analysis.

Critical Ethnography

Critical theorists believe that research is an ethical and political act (Apple, 1990; Biklen and Bodkin, 1998; Carspecken, 1996; Kincheloe and McLaren, 1998). Critical research is intended to engage and benefit those who are marginalized in society. Along these lines, critical research can best be understood in the context of the empowerment of individuals (McLaren, 1994). Inquiry that aspires to be called critical must be connected to an attempt to confront the injustice of a particular society or sphere within a society. Research thus becomes a transformative endeavor unembarrassed by the label "political" and unafraid to consummate a relationship with an emancipatory consciousness (Carspecken, 1996; Kincheloe and McLaren, 1998).

Critical researchers often regard their work as a first step toward forms of political action that can redress the injustices found in the field site or constructed in the very act of research itself. Thus critical researchers enter into an investigation with their assumptions on the table, so no one is confused about the epistemological and political baggage they bring with them to the research site.

Critical research considers education to be a social institution designed for social and cultural reproduction and transformation (Merriam, 1998). Drawing from Marxist philosophy, critical theory, and feminist theory, knowledge generated through this mode of research is an ideological critique of power, privilege, and oppression in areas of educational practice.

A critical ethnography of education, then, is a form of critical qualitative research that studies the multiple cultures of a school community (Biklen and Bodkan, 1998; Carspecken, 1996; Denzin and Lincoln, 1998). Ethnographic techniques become the strategies that critical researchers use to collect data about schooling practices and their relation to the social order, to ultimately undermine or transform that order (Carspecken, 1996). Employing a cultural studies epistemology that draws upon Marxism, postmodernism, and critical theory, I seek to avoid the pitfalls of sociological objectivity and functionalism, while giving room to the critical voices of urban youth that are often absent from traditional research. In essence, I agree with Kincheloe and McLaren (1998) that a Marxist-inspired critical ethnography deepened by a critical engagement with new currents of postmodern social theory has an important if not crucial role to play in the project of challenging and transforming oppressive and marginalizing educational practices and ultimately constructing new forms of socialist democracy.

Description of the Sample

Selection and Description of the Focal Site

I selected Pacific Beach High School as a focal site for several reasons. For several years, the school had been involved in a partnership with a major research university and, as part of that partnership, teachers, students, and administrators were involved in critical dialogue that questioned many assumptions underlying traditional high school practices. Also, the established collaboration between the university, the high school, and the community and the existence of the Pacific Beach Project allowed me easy access to students, classrooms, teachers, and the school as a whole. Investigation, evaluation, and reflection were major parts of the culture at Pacific Beach. Finally, Pacific Beach, as a high school almost evenly divided between rich and poor and students of color and students from the dominant group, provided a unique site for analysis.

Nestled along southern California's Pacific coast, Pacific Beach is a comprehensive high school with an enrollment of 3100 students. Hailed as a school with a population that closely reflects the demographics of the State of California, Pacific Beach has the following ethnic breakdown: 46.9% white, 32.6% Hispanic, 12.7% African-American, and 6.9% Asian. Four hundred and fifteen of the students are listed as "English learners," the overwhelming majority being Spanish speakers (298). Out of all Pacific Beach graduates, 67.8% are eligible for admission to the state's public universities as opposed to the 36.6% statewide average. A significant percentage (24.1%) of the students also qualifies to receive free or reduced meals. Sixty-six percent of the teachers at Pacific Beach are white, 17% are Hispanic, 8% African-American, and 6% Asian. The average SAT score for Pacific Beach High is 1048 compared to a state average of 1011 and a national average of 1016. (California Department of Education website)

Although these numbers seem to show that Pacific Beach is a successful or, at least above average school by traditional criteria, there exist huge disparities in achievement between students according to ethnic and socioeconomic background. The disparities are so great that Pacific Beach High School is often referred to as two schools, one highly successful campus that services the affluent population (which is largely composed of white and Asian-American students who are residents of the northern portion of the city), and another, less successful urban school that services the low-income (African-American and Latino) students who either live in the Rivera corridor, the poorest section of the city, or commute on permit from south Los Angeles.

Pacific Beach city and school district are so unique and complicated that I have dedicated chapter 4 to unpacking the history, political economy, and cultural politics of the city and their impact on academic achievement. In addition, I describe how the Pacific Beach Project was designed and implemented to combat the "two-school" phenomenon. At this point, it is important to simply emphasize that all the project participants and focal students were members of the "second school" as low-income students of color who either resided either in or near the Rivera corridor or commuted to campus from impoverished and working-class neighborhoods throughout the greater Los Angeles area.

Description of Participants

The participants in this study included:

- twenty-seven students of color who were all representatives of groups that had performed poorly at the school and were seen as members of the second school at Pacific Beach High;
- a team of four teachers, all of whom had roles at the university either as supervisors in the teacher education program or as graduate student researchers. Additionally, there was a parent bilingual community liaison from Pacific Beach High who worked with both the students and the university research team; and
- a university research team, composed of two senior faculty members, two full-time researchers, and four graduate students (not including the Pacific Beach teachers who were also enrolled in graduate programs), who also worked with students, parents, teachers, and school and district administrators.

The student participants were involved in a project involving collaboration between university faculty, graduate students, and educators at Pacific Beach High to examine and intervene in the trajectories students of color follow from the beginning of high school into their futures as citizens, community members, and workers. Toward these ends, the intervention/study was originally built around a ninth-grade humanities class at Pacific Beach High. Students in the Pacific Beach Project (PBP) became both researchers and research subjects over the course of their four-year involvement, participating in two major summer research seminars held at the university as well as carrying out several research projects as part of their coursework in the project classes at school.

Selection and Description of Focal Students

I was involved with the project for a few months before I felt comfortable selecting a purposeful yet typical sample of focal students (Berg, 2001: Biklen and Bodkan, 1998; Merriam, 1998). I ultimately decided to select students who were involved in the project activities that related to the critical study of popular cultures, and reflective of the range of academic achievement in the class. One student had, at the time I met her, a higher than 3.0 grade point average (GPA), one student between a 2.5 and a 3.0 GPA, and two students between a 2.0 and 2.5 GPA. The focal students also reflected the class with respect to gender and ethnic distribution, socioeconomic status, neighborhood of residence, home environment, and college aspirations. It is important, however, to note the conspicuous absence of African-American males and the 3:1 ratio of females to males among the focal students, as both of these inequities were reflected in the overall classroom population.

My choices were conscious ones reflecting the project population and trends at the school. While the lack of participation of males of color in academic programs is a serious issue that the project did address, it would have been a misrepresenta-

TABLE 1. Residence and Background of Focal Students

Name[1]	Ethnic Identity[2]	GPA[3]	Year Joined the Project	Neighborhood of Residence	Socioeconomic Background
Jaime Aguilar	Chicano	2.6	10th Grade	Rivera	Low-income
Luz Cavassa	Chicana	3.1	9th Grade	Rivera	Low-income
Imani Waters	African-American	2.3	9th Grade	San Fernando Valley	Low-income
Wanda Daniels	African-American	2.1	9th Grade	South LA/ Rivera	Low-income

1. All the names are pseudonyms.
2. I used designations that were in accordance with the ways in which the students self-identified.
3. These were the grade point averages at the time each was selected as a focal student. The GPAs are based on a 4.0 scale, though students are able to earn higher grade point averages with the extra points for Honors and Advanced Placement classes.

tion of reality to include them equally in the selection of focal students. The most salient criteria in the selection of focal students were that they reflected the ethnic, gender, socioeconomic, and academic distribution of the class and that they were involved in the activities related to the critical study of popular culture.

Jaime Aguilar. Jaime was a second-generation Chicano student with a cumulative grade point average of 2.6 in "regular" (non-Honors or Advanced Placement) courses. Jaime lived in an apartment close to the high school in the Rivera corridor with his mother and would be classified as low-income. During the two years of the study, I never knew him to mention his father, except to say that he had not been around. He did, however, have an adult male mentor from a "big brother" type program. This mentor attended many of Jaime's presentations and I conversed with him on several occasions.

Jaime joined the project at the end of his freshman year. According to his own testimony, he was aimless that first year and ran with the wrong crowd. Jaime frequently recalled an incident when he and a friend were chased by rival gang members through the streets near his home. "It was then," he would later say, "that I knew I needed to turn things around, that I was going nowhere." By the time I met Jaime, he was attempting to turn things around for himself. He had managed to raise his grades from Cs and Ds to a respectable grade point average. According to Mr. Genovese, the project teacher, Jaime still had difficulty shaking the tough-guy stereotype and dealing with teachers who didn't expect much from him. At the end of his sophomore year, many faculty members at Pacific Beach saw Jaime as having only marginal literacy skills.

Luz Cavassa. Luz was a second-generation Chicana student with a 3.1 grade point average in the "regular" courses at Pacific Beach. Luz was one of only five students in the project who managed to navigate her first two years of Pacific Beach with a GPA higher than 3.0. She lived in a small, low-income apartment close to the high school in the Rivera corridor with her parents and three younger siblings. As her parents worked long hours, Luz spent a great deal of time and energy looking after her younger sisters. She was intent on being a good role model for her siblings and helping to ensure their academic success. Luz was the only of the four focal students on a definite four-year college trajectory when I met her, though she was not enrolled in the highest track at Pacific Beach. She joined the project at the beginning of her freshman year and was considered "unofficially" as one of the project leaders among the students.

Although Luz held a GPA above 3.0, she had not completed any honors courses in the 9th or 10th grade. In fact, she had dropped out of an Honors English class in the 10th grade because she felt like an outsider and lacked confidence in her writing ability. At the time of the 1999 Summer Research Seminar, she was considering a second attempt at Honors/Advanced Placement English but was quite insecure about her ability to succeed.

Imani Waters. Imani was an African-American female with a grade point average of 2.3. She lived in a working-class neighborhood in the San Fernando Valley with her mother, older brother, and her mother's new husband. Imani's mother, who attended Pacific Beach, but dropped out before finishing at an alternative school, worked at a hospital near Pacific Beach and drove her daughter to school daily. Imani's older brother also attended and dropped out of Pacific Beach High. He was attending a junior college in the valley, where he was, in Imani's words, "getting by."

Imani was aware that her high school grades were not reflective of her academic ability, and she held high expectations for herself despite her less than stellar academic record. These high expectations were frequently countered, however, by spells of self-doubt and depression. Several of her teachers felt that she had potential, but most saw her as an extremely articulate young woman who could speak well but lacked basic academic reading and writing skills.

Wanda Daniels. Wanda was an African-American with a 2.1 GPA who vacillated between a house in a working-class neighborhood in southern Los Angeles and an apartment in the Rivera corridor of Pacific Beach. These residences belonged to her aunts, who took joint responsibility for her in the absence of any other guardians. Only occasionally would Wanda mention a mother or father and, when she did, it was only to say that they had not been around for her. Wanda also held a variety of after-school jobs at local eateries that would keep her occupied until late in the evening, thereby severely impacting her ability to complete her schoolwork. Mr. Genovese repeatedly talked with both aunts, who each believed that Wanda needed to work at her evening jobs.

Wanda joined the project at the beginning of her freshman year. She was a core member participating in most of the academic and social activities of the project. Although she was viewed as an amiable student who "worked hard," teachers outside the project perceived her as a student with limited literacy skills and abilities. By the end of her sophomore year, Wanda's cumulative grade point average, at 2.1, was the lowest among the focal students.

Selection and Description of Focal Teachers

For my analysis I chose to focus on two teachers, Mr. Genovese and Ms. Weiss, who had the greatest long-term involvement with the students and the project. Both were tenured faculty at Pacific Beach High who had worked at the school for a number of years and were respected by the administration and their faculty peers. Both were also active participants in the research community at the Graduate School of Education.

Mr. Genovese was the lead teacher in the project and ending his first year as a graduate student in the department of the graduate school of education where I was working as a research associate. He actually enrolled in graduate school during the second year of the project at the behest of several other graduate students who were also working on the project. As the lead teacher, he was responsible for teaching the project class at Pacific Beach for each of the four years that the students were involved. Mr. Genovese was also an active participant in each of the two summer research seminars.

Ms. Weiss was an accomplished English teacher at Pacific Beach High who taught English 11 and English 11 Advanced Placement (AP). She worked only half-time at Pacific Beach because the university had bought out the other half of her contract. During the mornings, Ms. Weiss was a high school English teacher. During the afternoons, she worked as a university field supervisor (UFS) and traveled from school to school providing mentoring and supervision to preservice English teachers. Ms. Weiss was also the district liaison for the Teacher Education Program and was responsible for securing all of the preservice teacher placements within the Pacific Beach district.

Data Collection

As a basis for my analysis, I generated the following sources of data:

- **Field notes.** During my involvement with the project, I recorded over 2,000 pages of observational notes. I observed the students in the practice of critical research where the creation, interpretation and interrogation of academic and popular texts were involved. My primary aim was to understand the impact of participation in a critical research community of practice on these students' ability to engage with existing texts and to create original texts that demonstrated academic and critical literacies. To this end, my notes captured the project participants in a variety of settings and activities. Depending on my level of engagement, I had varying strategies for taking the notes. In classroom observations where I was not directly involved in instruction, I was able to sit off to the side and take notes in a traditional manner. I was also able to take traditional notes when students were making presentations on their research. There were, however, many activities in which I was an active participant and stopping to take notes was not an option. There were other instances when taking notes would have been unnatural or conspicuous given my relationship with the students. On these occasions, I would write down my notes immediately after the event. My general rule was to preserve the natural flow of events and capture relevant data without compromising my role as a participant in the project.

- **Digital video and audio tape recordings and digital photography.** Frequently, I used digital video and audio equipment to collect data without disrupting events or curtailing my involvement. The camera was often set off to the side, and students and other project participants became used to its presence. I also used the video and photographic equipment to capture unique literacy events in non-traditional settings such as rallies, marches, assemblies, and other urban settings where the students were conducting their research (Hamilton, 2000). The recording equipment also became a research tool for the students to collect data for their own projects.

- **Transcriptions of Internet conversations.** I logged all of the interactions that I had with students over the Internet via either e-mail or AOL Instant Message and documents containing student work that were sent as attachments over the Internet or were printed out and given to me by the students. I also kept a log of all meeting notes and informal conversations relating to the students and the project that were carried over the Internet.

- **Examples of written student work**. Separate from the oral presentations, examples of student work included notes, essays, speeches, research papers, PowerPoint slides and examinations. The student work was collected in English and Social Studies classes at Pacific Beach as well as in the two Summer Research Seminars.

- **Interviews.** I interviewed the focal teachers, the focal students, university faculty, and full-time researchers associated with the project. The interviews with teachers were used to ascertain their individual philosophies on the critical study of popular culture as a way to facilitate the development of academic and critical literacies. Teacher philosophy and attitude will undoubtedly play a major role in the ultimate success of making the bridge between popular culture and the traditional curriculum. Also, I wanted to understand each teacher's motivation for making the decision to incorporate popular culture and to hear her or his own assessment of the effectiveness of the curriculum. The interviews with focal students were used to flesh out these issues in further detail as well as permit the students to evaluate the effectiveness of the curricula by their own criteria.

Utilizing the critical ethnographic method, I was able to collect meaningful data from multiple observations and conversations with students that I knew intimately over a period of over twenty months. This method allowed the ability to contextualize the data that were collected in each portion of this study. Also, I was able to triangulate the data by juxtaposing interviews with formal and informal observations as well as obtaining oral, written, and electronic evidences of student work.

Description of Categories for Analysis

As the goal of this study is to determine the impact of the critical study of popular culture on the development of academic and critical literacy, I centered my conceptual framework upon literacy events and literacy practices. Heath (1983) originally defined a literacy event as, "a communication act that represents any occasion in which a piece of writing is integral to the nature of participants' interactions and their interpretive processes." In subsequent years, several theorists (Barton and Hamilton, 2000; Ferdman, 1990; Gee, 1996; Mahiri, 1998; Street, 1993) as well as professional literacy organizations such as the National Reading Conference (Alvermann, 2001), the National Council of Teachers of English (NCTE/IRA, 1996), and the International Reading Association (NCTE/IRA, 1996) have argued for a broader definition of literacy that includes relevance to sociocultural contexts and technological advances. Barton and Hamilton (2000, p. 7) identify literacy practices as the general cultural ways of utilizing written language which people draw upon in their lives. The present study draws upon the concepts of literacy events and literacy practices in order to evaluate students' use of written language and other texts in their participation as critical researchers. I was most interested in student interactions with existing texts and students' production of original texts.

The categories for analysis were derived from a combination of literacy theory, critical theory, cultural theory, social theory, state and federal frameworks for English language arts and social studies, conversations with university faculty and administration, and materials relating to the advanced placement examinations in English language and composition, English literature, United States government, and economics. The categories I used to capture students' engagement with popular cultural and academic texts included the following: debating, critiquing, clarifying, assisting, problematizing, politicizing, and contemporizing. Throughout the research process, I also looked for examples of students taking ownership of and appropriating the tools and discourses of the academy.

I decided to focus on literacy events that featured students bridging popular cultural texts and academic texts or concepts; discussing academic texts or concepts; relating popular cultural texts to their everyday lives; and utilizing the academic texts or concepts to analyze everyday issues. All of the categories I utilized in analyzing data spoke to a critical understanding of or engagement with texts. Also, they signified students' confidence in their knowledge or mastery of the text. They also demonstrated that the students had "demystified" the academic text in their discussion and saw their reservoir of popular cultural knowledge as on an equal plane with "academic" knowledge. This is evidenced particularly in students' discussions of academic texts and in references to academic texts in their critical analyses of everyday culture. It was clear that, when using popular culture and their own experiences to enhance an argument or debate about an academic text, these students saw the knowledge that they had gained in their own personal experience as worthy of use in a theoretical discussion. Finally, all the chosen categories demonstrated a proficiency in the development of academic and critical literacies.

Social Location of the Researcher

Popular cultural practices in the postindustrial, postmodern urban landscape have defined my adolescent and adult life. Initially, I was a core participant in and member of a marginalized urban youth culture that used popular texts as a lens through which to view the world. Later, I became a teacher of urban students who held a similar worldview. I began my teaching career in East Bay City, an urban center in Northern California, in 1993 at the age of 22 and taught there for six years. During my final three years at East Bay, I taught half-time while I was enrolled in a doctoral program in education at a nearby university. While at East Bay, I taught 11th- and 12th-grade English, sponsored the African-American student union, coached varsity cross-country, basketball, and track and field, and sat on numerous department- and school-wide committees. During the summer of 1999, I moved from the Bay Area to Los Angeles and, within a week, was involved with the Pacific Beach Project students. I remained with the Pacific Beach project for more than two years.

I was born in the city where East Bay High is located and spent my early years in an urban neighborhood of the city. My father was a minister in this neighborhood for 17 years, and my mother has taught pre-school and kindergarten here for over 25 years. My grandmother, aunts, uncles, and numerous cousins also live in this city and, for most of the six years that I was teaching in the district, I lived within a mile of the high school. I say this because I had a vested interest in the success of urban students and an intimate knowledge of and involvement with the community and the school. I took this same commitment and these same sensibilities with me to Pacific Beach and they have defined my relationship with the students in the project.

As an African-American youth growing up in a metropolitan area during the 1970s and 1980s, I was very much a part of the emergent hip-hop culture, which, although not yet the commercial success it would come to be, played a dominant role in the identity of many African-Americans. I know that for me, after hearing one song at the age of nine, hip-hop became my favorite musical genre and it has been so ever since.

From junior high school through college, my world revolved around hip-hop culture and music. This included my haircut, my dress, my language, and, of course, my walk. This is not to mention the countless hours spent consuming music videos and learning new dances. It was around hip-hop that I first became politicized, watching Spike Lee's "Do the Right Thing" and listening to Public Enemy's "Fight the Power" during my senior year of high school. I was also known to wear an assortment of Africa medallions in honor of the motherland and the struggles of Nelson Mandela and the African National Congress. This, too, was part of the culture. The summer after graduation, I read Alex Haley's *Roots* in its entirety. This was one of the first books that I ever read cover to cover, and it was largely attributable to my inspiration from the Spike Lee film that I repeatedly watched and referenced via the hip-hop soundtrack released during that summer.